# HARDY:
## AN ILLUSTRATED DICTIONARY

# HARDY:

## AN ILLUSTRATED DICTIONARY

Alan Hurst

KAYE & WARD · LONDON
ST. MARTIN'S PRESS · NEW YORK

First published in Great Britain by
Kaye & Ward Ltd
21 New Street, London EC2M 4NT
1980

First published in the U.S.A. by
St. Martin's Press Inc.,
175 Fifth Avenue,
New York, N.Y. 10010
1980

ISBN 0 7182 1245 2 (Great Britain)
ISBN 0-312-36220-X (U.S.A.)

Library of Congress Catalog Card No. 80-5157

Set, printed and bound in Great Britain by
Fakenham Press Limited, Fakenham, Norfolk

# PREFACE

This volume is intended to provide a source of basic information about Hardy and, through the dictionary form, present an impression of the man and his work. Each novel has a separate entry giving details of composition and publication followed by a brief critical description and references to significant theatrical, film or television versions. Each volume of short stories and each volume of poetry is also represented as are a wide selection of individual stories and poems. Hardy's major characters and all his heroines are also included. Other entries are concerned with Hardy's life, relatives and contemporaries; with creative artists who influenced, or were influenced by him; with places connected with his life and work; with relevant critical or technical terms and with other aspects of his life likely to be of interest. The volume also includes: a special Appendix on Wessex; a finding list for Hardy's characters; a chronology and some suggestions for further reading.

Hardy wrote something on almost every day of his long literary career, read and studied continually and knew a remarkable number of people. A compiler of a Hardy dictionary faces the responsibility of selection. I apologize for my omissions in the knowledge that at least some of them, in Hardy's phrase, 'had to be'.

The illustrations are chosen not only to accompany specific entries but also to express the highly visual and 'photogenic' nature of Hardy's world. I would like to acknowledge the expert assistance of my brother, Jeff Hurst, in assembling the photographs. I would also like to thank Gregory Stevens Cox for his knowledgeable suggestions and assistance and, finally, my wife Joanne for her good-humoured support and perceptive criticisms of the manuscript.

*Cross referencing by the use of an asterisk has been included where it is felt that the reader might wish to refer to another entry in the dictionary or appendix for further information.*

# ACKNOWLEDGEMENTS

The author and publisher would like to thank Macmillan, London and Basingstoke, for permission to quote from *The Life of Thomas Hardy* by Florence Emily Hardy.

Photographs and Illustrations: Stevens-Cox, cover, pages 19,23, 25, 36, 49, 65, 68, 70, 71, 72, 73, 74, 75, 78, 96, 97, 101, 104, 113, 117, 122, 127, 137, 146, 148, 176, 194; Jeffrey Hurst, pages 17, 20, 27, 31, 32, 35, 43, 44, 48, 53, 64, 91, 102, 105, 111, 115, 131, 150, 162, 171, 173, 175, 185, 191, 195, 198; Dorchester County Museum, pages 10, 15, 38, 68, 69, 70, 75, 80, 81, 123, 125, 127, 136, 156, 166, 199; Alan Hurst, pages 16, 23, 62, 85, 90, 124, 138, 141, 166, 178, 188, 189, 192; E.M.I. Films, cover, pages 21, 58, 118, 161; Julian Morrell Vinogradoff, pages 61, 95, 112, 179; Imperial War Museum, pages 11, 108, 142, 169; B.B.C., pages 55, 83, 88, 106; Radio Times Hulton Picture Library, pages 86, 99, 100, 133; National Portrait Gallery, pages 95, 0153; Heron Books, pages 107, 167; the Virginia Woolf Estate, pages 50, 149; Salisbury Playhouse, pages 140, 165; Sir Robert Cooke, page 114; The Royal Photographic Society, pages 24, 121; London Borough of Camden, page 89; David Inshaw, page 129; Roger Mayne, page 160; Charles P. Friel, page 135; National Monuments Record, Crown Copyright Reserved, page 170; The Stone Collection, Birmingham Reference Library, page 92; The British Library, page 154; Society of Antiquaries of London, page 12; Burrill Productions, page 46; Mrs Gertrude Bugler, page 26; Her Majesty the Queen for Roger Fenton's photograph of 'The Victory', page 162.

Map of Wessex on page 184 by Bill Pinder.

# CONTENTS

# A

**Afterwards.** Hardy in his 77th year concluded *Moments of Vision**
with this poem telling how he hoped to be remembered as a man
who noticed not only the immensities of wintry constellations but
also the tiny hedgehog travelling furtively across the lawn on a
summer evening. It has been set to music by Christopher Le Flem-
ing in *Six Country Songs* (1936).

**Agnosticism.** Hardy's intellect, influenced by such works as *On
Liberty* by John Stuart Mill* and *The Origin of Species* by Charles
Darwin* led him, along with many Victorian contemporaries, to
abandon the inherited Christian beliefs of his childhood. He
remained emotionally attached to them and the conflict between his
scepticism and his religious feelings made him a deeply divided
person. In *Tess of the D'Urbervilles*,* Angel Clare* and his brothers
read a chapter of *A Counterblast to Agnosticism* every day during their
walking tour.

**Ainsworth, William Harrison** (1805–82). A romantic historical
novelist whose grandiose Gothic* melodramas fascinated the
young Hardy and had some influence in a small way on his own
writing.

**Aldclyffe, Cytherea** (*Desperate Remedies*). A wealthy and imperi-
ous older woman. Hardy compares her life to tropical nature, 'with
her hurricanes and the subsequent luxuriant vegetation effacing the
ravages'. She employs the daughter of her former lover and falls
jealously in love with her. She tries to live vicariously through the
young girl but is destroyed by her own intrigues.

**Aldeburgh.** A small town on the Suffolk coast, once a prosperous
seaport until subjected to the sea's encroachment. It is now famous
for an annual music festival. Hardy, a frequent visitor to Aldeburgh
as guest of Edward Clodd,* enjoyed 'the sensation of having
nothing between you and the North Pole'.

**Alicia's Diary.** The events of this high–Victorian short story move
with terrible swiftness between the Bronte-like atmosphere of
Wherryborne rectory and the glitter of Venice.* Alicia remains at

Thomas Hardy and Edward Clodd at Aldeburgh c. 1909.

home while her sister Caroline visits France and becomes engaged to a painter, Charles de la Feste. When he comes to England he falls in love with Alicia and conspires to save Caroline from despair by contracting a false marriage to her. Events compel him to validate the marriage and soon afterwards he drowns himself. Five years later Caroline marries the Rev. Theophilus Higham and Alicia is left to recall the time 'when life shone more warmly in my eye than it does now'. Hardy wrote *Alicia's Diary* after his 1887 visit to Italy and collected it in *A Changed Man* (1913).★

**Allusions.** Hardy displays his acquired knowledge, sometimes pedantically, through allusions in his novels to art, history, contemporary figures, or the like: Eustacia Vye's★ presence, in *The Return of the Native*,★ 'brought memories of such things as Bourbon roses, rubies, and tropical midnights; her moods recalled lotuseaters and the march in "Athalie" . . .'; Bathsheba Everdene★ in *Far From the Madding Crowd*★ is 'an Elizabeth in brain and a Mary Stuart in spirit'. Hardy's allusions at other times increase the clarity and effectiveness of the pictures: in *The Well-Beloved,*★ 'the raw rain flies level as the missiles of the ancient inhabitants across the beaked promontory'.

**Ancestry.** Hardy took a lifelong interest in genealogy. He compiled a family tree tracing the paternal side of his family to the fifteenth century le Hardys of Jersey and the maternal side to Anglo-Saxon small-holders of north-west Dorset.* The Hardys showed, 'all the characteristics of an old family of spent social energies' and the theme of family decline emerges strongly in *Tess of the D'Urbervilles.** The record of illegitimacy, hasty marriage and bitter feuds on both sides of the family gave him a feeling of family curse. He died childless.

**Animals.** Hardy's love of animals and his horror of all forms of cruelty to them inspired his life-long campaign against bloodsports, vivisection and the use of animals in war.* He regarded nature* as an organic unity and did not differentiate sharply between man and beast. Many poems reflect this view and the vitality of his characters* also stems from it: Tess Durbeyfield* is seen as warm 'as a sunned cat'; the piglet in *Jude the Obscure,** who escapes his alien purchaser, speeds 'with all the agility his little legs afforded ... following an unerring line towards his old home'.

Pack-horses being loaded in the Great War.

**Annotations.** The dated marginal notes to various passages in Hardy's bibles and prayer book show his intimate knowledge of the scriptures and provide a useful source of biographical information.

**Antell, John** (1816–78). Hardy's uncle, a Puddletown* shoemaker, who taught himself Latin but whose dreams of going to college were ruined by poverty and drunkenness. He is said to have been partly the model for Jude Fawley★ in *Jude the Obscure*.

**Anthologies.** Anthologies of Hardy's verse include selections by T. R. M. Creighton, P. N. Furbank, James Gibson, Geoffrey Grigson, Trevor Johnson, John Crowe Ransom, John Wain, Carl Weber, W. E. Williams, David Wright and G. M. Young. None of Hardy's poems is without its particular interest and it is difficult to select and arrange them satisfactorily in anthology form. Most anthologists present their selections either chronologically or thematically and contain helpful introductions. G. M. Young, in his introduction, sees Hardy the poet as 'an ageing man watching the fire die down, and thinking of old tunes, old memories: moments remembered at railway stations and lodging houses; sunsets at the end of London streets, water coming over the weir, the rain on the downs'.

**Arch, Joseph** (1826–1919). Self-taught son of a shepherd who became a Methodist lay preacher and later Liberal Member of Parliament. He lived in Warwickshire and agitated against the poor conditions of agricultural labourers, organizing them into trade-unions which achieved some improvements. During one of his tours of Dorset★ Hardy heard him speak and in *The Dorsetshire Labourer*★ praises the commonsense, good humour, and moderation of his speeches.

**Archaeology.** Hardy's interest in archaeology was nourished by

A defender's backbone pierced by a Roman arrowhead in the 'Battle of the East Gate' at Maiden Castle, AD 44–43.

local excavations and discoveries including those at Max Gate★ of three ancient graves containing neatly enclosed skeletons. 'It was impossible to dig more than a foot or two deep about the town fields without coming upon some tall soldier or other of the Empire, who had lain there in his silent unobtrusive rest for the space of fifteen hundred years.' (*The Mayor of Casterbridge*★) cf. *Some Romano-British Relics*.★

**Archer, William** (1856–1924). Dramatic critic, editor, and translator of Ibsen's★ plays, whose 'Real Conversations' (1904) includes an interview with Hardy. In his review of 'Wessex Poems' Archer described Hardy's 'seeing all the words of the dictionary on one plane' and Hardy expressed his pleasure at the comment. (Letter to Archer, 21 December 1898.)

**Architecture.** In 1856 Hardy was apprenticed to a kind and scholarly local architect, John Hicks, of 39 South Street, Dorchester.★ For the next 16 years architecture was a major concern of his working life, overlapping and influencing his literary career. He

King's Cross Station, built 1851–2 as the terminal of the Great Northern Railway.

worked intermittently as a Gothic* draughtsman, restoring and designing churches.* While working on the restoration of St Juliot* Church, Cornwall, in 1870, he met his first wife, Emma Lavinia Gifford.* Later he designed his own house, Max Gate,* near Dorchester. *The Architectural Notebook of Thomas Hardy* (Dorset Natural History and Archaeological Society, 1966) contains plans for water closets and drainage systems and shows Hardy's involvement with the Victorian architect's dilemma – how to reconcile stone and iron, architecture and engineering. The railway* station, meeting place of Victorian architecture and engineering, features prominently in Hardy's world. In *Jude the Obscure** Sue Bridehead* says, 'I'd rather sit in the railway station ... That's the centre of town life now. The Cathedral has had its day!'

**Arnold, Matthew** (1822–88). Victorian poet, critic and educationist dedicated to preserving culture against philistinism and adapting religion* to modern thought. Hardy, on Leslie Stephen's* advice, read Arnold extensively. Although there is no evidence of direct influence, Arnold's 'disease of modern life' is echoed in 'the ache of modernism' felt by Hardy's characters (cf. Paula Power* and Jude Fawley*). In later years Hardy rejected Arnold's attempt to have dogma 'balanced on its feet by hairsplitting', as they both observed the crumbling of belief in Christianity.

**Auden, Wystan Hugh** (1907–73). A modern English poet, critic, librettist, anthologist and much-travelled 'citizen of the world' who led the politically-committed poets of the thirties and later moved towards a religious standpoint. His verse is intellectualized, sometimes didactic, technically brilliant. In the essay 'A Literary Transference' (1940) Auden celebrated Hardy, his 'poetic father', for his 'hawk's vision, his way of looking at life from a very great height'.

# B

**Ballad.** A story from homely or familiar materials, economically told, which creates a sense of mystery. The ballad, originally sung, is firmly rooted in a popular oral tradition and is an important influence on Hardy's art.

**Barnes, William** (1801–86). William Barnes, son of a Dorset

farmer, took holy orders and eventually became rector of Winterborne Came.★ Schoolmaster, archaeologist, philologist and poet,
he was Hardy's teacher, cherished friend and inspirer. His unaffected poems, written in dialect,★ give restful pictures of country
life. In October 1879, Hardy wrote an unsigned review for *New
Quarterly* of Barnes' *Poems of Rural Life in the Dorset Dialect*. After
Barnes' death he wrote an obituary in *Athenaeum* (1886) and a poetic
tribute *The Last Signal*.★ Later he edited *Select Poems of William
Barnes*★ (1908) with a preface and glossorial notes. Hardy's admiration for Barnes' poetry cannot be overestimated and it provided a
powerful touchstone for his own poetry in its blend of joy and
sorrow. 'Smile on, happy maidens! but I shall noo mwore / Zee the
maid I do miss under evenen's dim sky'. To suggestions that his
dialect-language would become obsolete he replied: 'To write in
what some may deem a fast outwearing speech-form may seem as
idle as the writing of one's name in snow on a spring day. I cannot
help it. It is my mother tongue ... the only true speech of the life
that I draw.'

 William Barnes.

**Barrie, Sir James Matthew** (1860–1937). Scottish novelist and dramatist, author of *The Admirable Crichton* (1902) and *Dear Brutus* (1917) but best known for *Peter Pan* (1904) which has become a childhood classic. Barrie, a friend of long standing, was at Max Gate★ when Hardy died, helped his widow to arrange the funeral at Westminster Abbey, and to revise and edit *The Life.*★

**Beaminster** (Emminster). A small town six miles north of Bridport,★ nestling beneath steep hills, 'Sweet Be'minster that bist abound / By green an' woody hills all round' (William Barnes★). Despite fires in 1864 and 1781 many mellow stone houses survive and the atmosphere remains as Hardy described it in *Tess.*★

**Beeny Cliff.** A huge blue-black cliff rising 200 feet above the sea on the north-eastern coast of Cornwall, near Boscastle,★ which Hardy often visited with Emma Lavinia Gifford★ while courting her. It is brilliantly described in *A Pair of Blue Eyes*★ as The Cliff with No Name. Revisiting the place 40 years later after Emma's death Hardy notes in the poem *Beeny Cliff,* that 'Still in all its chasmal beauty bulks old Beeny to the sky' but it speaks to him only of her absence. The poem receives a fine commentary from Donald Davie in 'Hardy's Virgilian Purples' (*Agenda,* 1972).

Beeny Cliff.

**Beerbohm, Sir Max** (1872–1956). Essayist, critic, short-story writer, and caricaturist who satirized social pretences and literary mannerisms. He entertainingly parodies Hardy in 'A Sequelula to "The Dynasts" by Th★m★s H★rdy' (1912), and gives an amusing account of the Prince of Wales' visit to Hardy in 1923 in the poem 'A Luncheon'.

**Bere Regis** (Kingsbere). A Dorset★ village, once an important mediaeval centre and resort of kings. The Saxon church, largely rebuilt in the fifteenth century, has a battlemented tower in chequered flint and stone. In the south aisle stands the Turberville vault with a square-arched Tudor window bearing the lion rampant of Tess's★ ancestors. The tragic chain of events in *Tess of the D'Urbervilles*★ begins when Parson Tringham tells John Durbeyfield, Tess's father, that his ancestors lie at Kingsbere, 'rows and rows of you in your vaults, with your effigies under Purbeck-marble canopies'.

The Turberville window at Bere Regis church.

**Besant, Walter** (1836–1901). Victorian man of letters who regarded *The Return of the Native*★ as 'the most original the most virile and most humorous of all modern novels' and invited Hardy to join the Rabelais Club.

**Betjeman, Sir John** (b. 1906). Poet Laureate with an enthusiasm for Victorian architecture★ and a horror of the vulgarities of modern life. His witty examination of the contemporary scene from an old-fashioned viewpoint has made him a best-selling poet. Betjeman's exceptionally strong sense of place links him to Hardy, cf. 'Dorset' and 'The Heart of Thomas Hardy' (*Collected Poems,* 1958) and his essay 'Hardy and Architecture' (*The Genius of Thomas Hardy,* 1976).

**Bibliography.** The standard bibliography is Richard L. Purdy's incomparable *Thomas Hardy: A Bibliographical Study* (1954). Helpful critical bibliographies are given in *Eight Modern Writers,* J. I. M. Stewart (1963), *Hardy's Vision of Man,* F. R. Southerington (1971), *Thomas Hardy: The Poetry of Perception,* Tom Paulin (1975).

**Bindon Abbey** (Wellbridge Abbey). A Cistercian Abbey half a mile east of Wool, founded in 1172 and now in ruins. The ancient tree-shaded fish-ponds, level grassed walks create an atmosphere of utter stillness. The empty stone coffin into which Angel Clare★ placed Tess★ in the sleep-walking scene of *Tess*★ can still be visited.

**Biography.** Hardy is proving an elusive subject for biographers. A very reticent and private man, he took steps to thwart biographers ('he resents other people fussing over something of his own which he cannot himself keep,' T. E. Lawrence★) by destroying some of his notebooks,★ letters, and diaries and writing his own 'ghosted' biography, *The Life.*★ Ernest Brennecke's gossipy *The Life of Thomas Hardy* (1925) had so infuriated him that he cabled the American publisher and threatened legal action.

Hardy biography remains a sensitive and controversial area as Dr Robert Gittings' recent two-volume biography, *Young Thomas Hardy* (1975) and *The Older Hardy* (1978), has demonstrated. This major work of great thoroughness and scope, in complete contrast to the earlier admiring portrait of Carl J. Weber, *Hardy of Wessex* (1940), presents a highly critical account of its subject. Gittings' biography of Hardy's second wife Florence,★ *The Second Mrs Hardy* (1979), written in collaboration with Jo Manton, presents an even bleaker portrait. In the Index for Hardy, his character is said to comprise 'hypochondria, self-absorption, stinginess, luxuriating in

Thomas Hardy, with Florence Hardy on his left, at a hospital fete opening, Dorchester, 20 July 1921.

misery, selfishness, inhospitality, susceptibility to young women, mother-fixation'. Gittings' biography may be seen in the context of the contemporary wish 'to see our great men at their worst as well as their best' (Richard Ellmann) and as a corrective to local hero-worship of the Wessex wizard which resents any criticism at all. There is also a tendency to examine every minute utterance or incident from Hardy's life so intensely that a sense of balance is lost.

The Gittings' biography has proved a creative catalyst in Hardy biography inviting *its* critics to substantiate their view of the man who wrote at the end of *The Return of the Native:*\* 'Some believed him, and some believed not; some said that his words were commonplace, others complained of his want of theological doctrine... But everywhere he was kindly received, for the story of his life had become generally known'.

**Birth.** Thomas Hardy was born on Tuesday morning 2 June 1840. The doctor pronounced him dead but the nurse; feeling a flicker of life, exclaimed, 'Dead! Stop a minute; he's alive enough, sure!'

**Birthplace.** A rambling seven-room thatched house at Higher Bockhampton,\* which was built for Hardy's grandfather in 1801.

Hardy's birthplace, Higher Bockhampton.

Hardy's earliest surviving poem 'Domicilium' describes how its secluded beauty merges completely with the surrounding countryside. Hardy's Cottage is now owned by the National Trust and open to the public.

**Blackmore, Richard Doddridge** (1825–1900). Poet and novelist, whose popular classic *Lorna Doone* (1869), prompted Hardy to write a congratulatory letter praising its 'exquisite ways of describing things which are more after my own heart than the "presentations" of any other writer that I am acquainted with'. (Letter, 8 June 1875.)

**Blomfield, Sir Arthur William** (1829–99). A distinguished church architect, son of a bishop of London, for whom Hardy worked as an assistant-architect in London from 1862–7. Hardy appreciated Blomfield's urbane influence and dedicated the poem 'Heiress and Architect' to him.

**Blunden, Edmund** (1896–1974). Poet, scholar, and critic who was introduced to Hardy by Siegfried Sassoon* and who, while holding a chair at Hong Kong University, did much to popularize Hardy's work in the Orient. cf. Blunden's *Thomas Hardy* (1942) and his monograph 'Guest of Thomas Hardy' (1964).

**Boldwood, William** (*Far From the Madding Crowd*). A fine-looking middle-aged tenant farmer, apparently a confirmed bachelor until receiving Bathsheba Everdene's★ frivolously sent valentine and being completely unmanned by a violent and possessive love ('If an emotion possessed him at all, it ruled him'). His desperate attempts to marry Bathsheba were near success when Sergeant Troy,★ her husband who was thought drowned, violently interrupted his engagement party. Boldwood seized a gun and shot dead his rival.

William Boldwood (Peter Finch) proposes to Bathsheba Everdene (Julie Christie) in the film *Far From the Madding Crowd*, 1967.

**Bonaparte, Napoleon** (1769–1821). Hardy's lifelong interest in Napoleon began when he was eight. He found in a closet a periodical covering the Napoleonic wars and was fascinated by its 'melodramatic prints of serried ranks, crossed bayonets, huge knapsacks, and dead bodies'. Hardy's prolonged researches into the struggle between Bonaparte and the English were expressed in *The Trumpet Major* (1880),★ *The Return of the Native* (1878),★ *A Tradition of 1804,*★ *The Melancholy Hussar*★ and, above all, *The Dynasts*★ (1904, 1906, 1908). In the latter work Napoleon is presented as a tyrant who is himself subject to the tyranny of the Immanent Will.

**Boscastle** (Castle Boterel). A tiny fishing village in north Cornwall two miles west of St Juliot★ which Hardy often visited while courting Emma Lavinia Gifford.★ In her memoirs, *Some Recollections*,★ Emma writes, 'Often we walked to Boscastle Harbour down the beautiful Valency valley where we had to jump over stones and climb over a low wall ... to come out on great wide spaces suddenly'. It is the location of a fine poem, 'At Castle Boterel', in which the primeval landscape is permanently identified with Hardy and Emma's visit.

**Boughton, Rutland** (1878–1960). A composer who set Hardy's *The Queen of Cornwall*★ to music. Hardy found him an interesting companion while not sharing his left-wing political views.

**Bournemouth** (Sandbourne). In 1810 Lewis Tregonwell built a holiday house on a wild moorland and by 1840 a marine village was established. Within 50 years the population had reached 37,000. The poem 'We Sat At The Window, Bournemouth, 1875' describes Hardy and Emma,★ after their first year of marriage, gazing at the rain from their hotel window with the appalling suspicion that they have nothing to say to each other. It is at a boarding house in Sandbourne that Tess★ murders Alec D'Urberville.★

**Bridehead, Sue** (*Jude the Obscure*). A dark-haired, nervous woman, full of new ideas, who tried to escape from tradition and conformity. She strongly attracted her cousin Jude Fawley★ and her elderly teacher Richard Phillotson★ although she herself was averse to sex. After a disastrous marriage to Phillotson she attempted to live an emancipated life with Jude; tragedy overtook them, Sue returned to Phillotson and Jude died. Although remaining 'a pert little thing with her tight-strained nerves', superficial, frigid, and stubborn, Sue Bridehead wins the sympathy of many readers for her 'advanced' views and life-style. For Hardy she was the 'type of woman which has always had an attraction for me' and she is partly modelled on Tryphena Sparks,★ Florence Henniker,★ and Emma Hardy★ (who regarded herself as 'bohemian'). D. H. Lawrence★ suggests that the female in her was 'subordinated to the male principle'. She is one of Hardy's most fascinating creations through whom he explored sexual neuroses much ahead of his time.

**Bridges, Robert** (1844–1930). A scholarly poet who achieved success with his philosophical 'The Testament of Beauty' (1929) and gave early recognition to the genius of Gerald Manley Hopkins. Hardy met Bridges several times but had a poor regard for his poetry.

**Bridport** (Port Bredy). An elegant town whose wide streets suggest 'at a glance that it has had a past' (Hermann Lea★) and end in tranquil views of green hills. The main street lined with Georgian buildings rises to the fine Town Hall where South Street intersects and leads to the port of West Bay one and a half miles to the south. Bridport continues its ancient rope and net-making industry. It is a town in Wessex★ for strange arrivals and departures and the main setting of the story *Fellow Townsmen.*★

(*Above*) Greyhound Hotel and Town Hall, Bridport, at the turn of the century.

(*Left*) Bridport today.

**British Museum.** During frequent visits to the British Museum Hardy studied the people he saw there as acutely as he did the museum's treasures. Crowds wandered gaily among the mummies, chatting flippantly, joking beneath Rameses the Great while Hardy pondered the consequences of such easy familiarity. The coughs of the visitors seemed to merge with ghostly coughs rising from the vaults. Hardy emerged in the evenings to notice with a shock the queues already forming outside the Music Halls.

Portrait of The British Museum by Roger Fenton.

**Britten, Benjamin** (1913–76). English composer and founder of the Aldeburgh★ Music Festival whose prolific works include many based on literary sources. His song-cycle *Winter Words* Op. 52 (1954) presents eight Hardy poems: 'At a Day Close in November', 'Midnight on the Great Western', 'Wagtail and Baby', 'The Little Old Table', 'The Choirmaster's Burial', 'Proud Songsters', 'At The Railway Station, Upway', 'Before Life and After'. These understated yet powerful songs were first sung by Peter Pears at the 1954 Festival.

**Browning, Robert** (1812–89). Victorian poet who eloped to Italy in 1846 with the invalid poetess Elizabeth Barrett after a clandestine marriage. Hardy met Browning in London and although suspicious of his optimism ('worthy of a dissenting grocer') admired his poetry.

**Bugler, Gertrude** (b. 1897). Beautiful Dorset girl whom Hardy first met in 1913 while she was rehearsing the part of Marty South. As a leading actress for the Hardy Players★ she gave memorable performances as Eustacia Vye★ (1920) and Tess★ (1924). Hardy thought her 'the very incarnation' of Tess and was deeply moved by her acting. He attended a special rehearsal of *Tess*★ at Woolbridge Manor,★ the original setting for the honeymoon scene. When in 1925 she was invited by Frederick Harrison to play Tess in London with a professional cast, Florence Hardy★ intervened and persuaded her to abandon the project lest Hardy should attempt the journey to London and overexcite himself. Happily she did go on to play Tess with great success in London in 1929.

It wasn't until 1964, in Blunt's biography of Sydney Cockerell, that she learnt of Hardy's supposed 'infatuation' with her – an interpretation of events which has gained widespread currency. Hardy's interest in her, however, was based on his perception of her

Gertrude Bugler as Tess with Norman Atkinson as Alec D'Urberville.

artistry and remarkable understanding of some of his heroines. Gertrude Bugler, now living in Beaminster,★ proudly recalls her association with Hardy, his kindliness and laughter, and vigorously rejects the portrait of him as a mean and gloomy man. After her last visit to Max Gate★ during Hardy's lifetime he told her, 'If anyone asks you if you knew Thomas Hardy, say, "Yes, he was my friend" '.

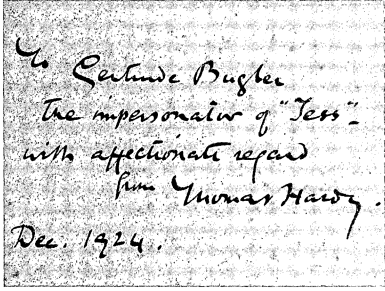

Hardy's inscription in Gertrude Bugler's copy of *Tess*.

**Burial.** On 26 January 1928, Hardy's ashes were ceremoniously buried in Poet's Corner, Westminster Abbey, in the presence of his second wife, Florence,★ the Prime Minister Stanley Baldwin, and a great crowd of dignitaries. Barrie,★ Gosse,★ Housman,★ Kipling, and Shaw were pallbearers. At the same hour his heart was buried at Stinsford★ under the yew tree in the grave of his first wife, Emma.★ Hardy would have appreciated the sombre ironies of this double burial.

**Byron, Lord George Gordon** (1788–1824). Romantic poet whose turbulent life and personality made him a legendary figure. Hardy signed a petition to admit Byron to Poet's Corner because, 'whatever Byron's bad qualities he was a poet and a hater of cant'.

Hardy's grave at Stinsford.

# C

**Candour in English Fiction.** An essay, published in *The New Review*, 1890, in which Hardy blamed low standards of contemporary fiction on prudish censorship and laws framed as social expedients without a basis in the heart of things. He wrote it during the controversy over the serial publication of *Tess.*★

**Cantle, Christian** (*The Return of the Native*). A nervous but lovable simpleton whom no woman would marry. The last one he asked said, 'Get out of my sight, you slack-twisted, slim-looking maphrotight fool,' which, as Timothy Fairway remarked, was hardly encouraging. He believed that Eusacia Vye★ was a witch.

**Carlyle, Thomas** (1795–1881). Scottish essayist, critic, political writer and thinker. Hardy read Carlyle over many years and maintained that his passage on the silent growth of the oak in *The French Revolution* (1837) had never been surpassed as a specimen of contemplative prose (*Fortnightly Review*, 1887).

27

**Carr, J. W. Comyns** (1849–1916). Critic and dramatist who collaborated with Hardy to produce a stage version of *Far From the Madding Crowd,*★ entitled *Mistress of the Farm* (1880), which was put in rehearsal by the management of St James's Theatre and then rejected.

**Cerne Abbas** (Abbot's Cernel). A beautifully sheltered village five miles north of Dorchester.★ The Cerne Giant, an 180 foot high figure of a naked man carved into the neighbouring hillside, is thought to be of Romano–British origin and associated with fertility rites. The tithe-barn at Cerne Abbas was Hardy's model for the 'great barn' in *Far From the Madding Crowd.*★

**Changed Man and Other Tales, A.** The stories in this volume – *A Changed Man, The Waiting Supper,*★ *Alicia's Diary,*★ *The Grave by the Handpost,*★ *Enter a Dragoon,*★ *A Tryst at an Ancient Earthwork,*★ *What the Shepherds Saw,*★ *A Committee-Man of the Terror,*★ *Master John Horseleigh Knight, The Duke's Reappearance,*★ *The Romantic Adventures of a Milkmaid*★ – were serialized individually before being collectively published by Macmillan at 6s. in an edition of 10,000 copies on 24 October 1913. The stories, often hastily written 'with a view to a fleeting life in a periodical', show both Hardy's relish for the eerie and the supernatural and his strong sense of place.

In *The Changed Man* (1901) readers familiar with the topography of Casterbridge and environs can exactly locate almost every scene from the opening shot of the view down Casterbridge High Street from Top 'o Town over Grey's Bridge. From there the white riband of road plunged 'into innumerable rustic windings, shy shades and solitary undulations up hill and down dale for 120 miles till it exhibited itself at Hyde Park Corner . . .'

The hussar captain Maumbry, influenced by the new curate's preaching, decides to leave the service and become a parson himself, 'a soldier – of the church militant'. The 'changed' man returns to a poor parish in Casterbridge and his broken-hearted young wife decides to leave him for another soldier, Lieutenant Vannicock. On their way past Casterbridge they find the Rev. Maumbry courageously fighting a cholera epidemic from which he dies. What happened to the lieutenant is not known 'but Mrs Maumbry lived and died a widow'.

**Chant, Mercy** (*Tess of the D'Urbervilles*). Mercy Chant, first seen wearing 'a broad-brimmed hat and highly starched cambric morning-gown, with a couple of books in her hand', is a devout churchworker. Angel Clare's★ parents hope he will marry her but he fiendishly whispers heretical ideas in her ear. She marries his more orthodox brother, Cuthbert.

**Characters.** Hardy's characters are firmly but simply drawn. The men fall into various categories: staunch worthies – Gabriel Oak,★ John Loveday,★ Diggory Venn,★ Giles Winterborne;★ reflective souls – Henry Knight,★ Clym Yeobright,★ Angel Clare;★ seducers – Sergeant Troy,★ Damon Wildeve,★ Edred Fitzpiers,★ Alec D'Urberville;★ loners – Michael Henchard,★ William Boldwood.★ The women★ achieve a wider range and psychological complexity and are realized with astonishing warmth and physicality. The men and women of Wessex★ are brought to life through action and dialogue rather than self-revelation or authorial description. They step from the page human and vulnerable: Gabriel Oak thumping his watch, Bathsheba Everdene★ glancing in her small mirror, William Boldwood nervously pacing his darkening stables, Sergeant Troy asleep in the church porch. They are often most themselves when most ridiculous. Many of them are too simple or too engaged in the toils of their plot to indulge in self-analysis. In contrast to his often unconvincing villains and high-society people, with their stilted language and melodramatic gestures, his good people are quite exceptionally interesting.

**Charmond, Mrs Felice** (*The Woodlanders*). An ex-actress who sought romantic diversions in a woodland mansion she found hateful ('I lay awake last night and I could hear the scrape of snails creeping up the glass of the window'). After scheming to win Dr Edred Fitzpiers★ she eloped with him to the Continent where she was shot dead by a former lover from South Carolina.

**Chesterton, Gilbert Keith** (1874–1936). Novelist, essayist, poet, critic and polemicist whose description of Hardy as 'a sort of village atheist brooding and blaspheming over the village idiot' (*The Victorian Age in Literature*, 1913) was, he later insisted, 'not meant derogatorily'. Hardy, in a passage omitted from *The Life*★ dismissed Chesterton as a 'phrasemongering literary contortionist'.

**Chickerel, Ethelberta** (*The Hand of Ethelberta*). A butler's daughter who successfully posed as a lady in 'manner, look, and accent', and married and mastered an aristocratic old roué, Lord Mountclere.

**Childhood among the Ferns.** Hardy wrote this exquisite poetic reminiscence when he was in his eighties – though possibly from an earlier draft-poem. The young Hardy sits alone beneath luxuriant tall-stemmed ferns during a summer shower observing his 'spray-roofed house' so intently that he escapes from self-consciousness into an imaginary world. Rain-drops pierce the green-rafters of his 'house' but he imagines he is not being rained upon. When the reality of the sun bursts through with actual warmth and sweetness he feels so happy that he wonders why he should have 'to grow to man's estate / And this afar-noised World perambulate?'

Hardy's longing for permanence, for time to stand still, was first recorded in *The Life*★ (p. 15); lying on his back in the sun he came to the conclusion that he did not want to grow up. (Jude Fawley★ expresses a similar wish at the beginning of *Jude the Obscure.*★) Hardy, the supreme observer, refuses involvement with the world on any terms but his own. The poem presents the tall ferns, the rain-drops, the sun's rays, the warm odours with startling immediacy. It is ironic that Hardy himself seems touchingly old sitting beneath the ferns: despite his assertion elsewhere that he felt a child till he was 16, a youth till he was 25, a young man till he was nearly 50 the poem invites the thought that he never had a childhood but was always 'old-fashioned'.

**Christmas Ghost-Story, A.** In this poem the ghost of an English soldier killed in the Boer War asks when Christianity was 'ruled inept and set aside' and why we bother to tack 'Anno Domini' to the years. Criticized in the *Daily Chronicle* (1889) for disloyalty to brave soldiers Hardy claimed Biblical and classical precedents for his ghost and justification for his condemnation of un-Christian conduct, especially at Christmas time. The editor conceded that one couldn't argue with a poet.

**Churches.** Churches in general, and Stinsford★ church in particular, occupy an important place in Hardy's life and work. Despite his agnosticism,★ these ancient repositories of tradition, ritual, prayer, and music★ abounded in comforting associations for him. He described himself as 'churchy' and churches often feature in his writing. Unlike T. S. Eliot's★ empty, secluded chapel in 'Little Gidding', remembered 'while the light fails / On a winter's after-noon' Hardy's churches invariably form the scene of some human drama. 'The two were silent in a sunless church ...' ('Her Dilemma'). Tess Durbeyfield loved the chanting in her church, despite the accusatory glances and whisperings of the unfriendly congregation.

Hardy was equally drawn to churchyards and carried a small

Stinsford.

Bincombe.

Loders.

Piddletrenthide.

knife with which to scrape the moss from the tomb-stones. On one sunny morning in October 1925 he recorded cleaning an inscription which read: 'Dear friend should you mourn for me / I am where you soon must be.'

**Clare, John** (1793–1864). English nature* poet who led an unsettled and poignant life in Northamptonshire and went tragically insane in 1837. His tough-minded realism,* hatred of injustice and oppression, and bluntness of language sprung from the same rural sources which nourished Hardy.

**Clodd, Edward** (1840–1930). Banker, author, and leading free-thinker who encouraged like-minded Victorians to gather at his home in Aldeburgh.* Hardy's friendship with Clodd was strained towards the end by a habit of churchgoing which baffled his rationalist friend. Clodd's final verdict was that Hardy, though a great writer, was 'not a great man; there was no largeness of soul'.

**Cockerell, Sir Sydney Carlisle** (1867–1962). Art connoisseur and collector, calligrapher, engraver, manuscript expert who became director of the Fitzwilliam Museum, Cambridge, in 1908. As Hardy's literary executor he supervised the distribution of manuscripts to various museums and assisted Hardy's widow in sorting out and burning papers at Max Gate.*

**Coggan, Jan** (*Far From the Madding Crowd*). A jovial farm-hand who was Bathsheba Everdene's* master-shearer and a staunch friend of Gabriel Oak.* He provided loyal companionship throughout Oak's troubles with Bathsheba and organized a belated celebration when they were eventually united. He took great delight in noting how quickly his friend took to saying 'my wife'.

**Collected Editions.** The first uniform and complete edition of Hardy's work 'The Wessex Novels' (16 vols.) was published by Osgood, McIlvaine & Co. 1895–6, with Hardy's revisions and a special preface for each novel. Macmillan became Hardy's sole publishers in 1902 and brought out the definitive 'Wessex Edition' (24 vols.) from 1912–31. This edition contained Hardy's final revisions and an important General Preface in which he explained his classification of the novels. The 'Mellstock Edition', a 'de-luxe' edition limited to 500 copies, was published 1919–20. 'The New Wessex Edition', in both hardback and paperback, with new introductions by leading Hardy scholars under the general editorship of P. N. Furbank, was published by Macmillan in 1974–5. Hardy's novels are now out of copyright.

**Collins, Vere H.** Educational manager of Oxford University Press who recorded five long conversations with Hardy between April 1920 and August 1922 (*Talks with Thomas Hardy*, 1928). The droll tone of the conversations is caught by the following exchange: 'HARDY: Stay as long as you like. Do not think of us, but only of your train. COLLINS: Thank you very much. HARDY: What train are you thinking of catching?'

**Collins, William Wilkie** (1824–89). He was called to the bar in 1851 but adopted literature as a profession. *The Woman in White* (1860) and *The Moonstone* (1868) were among the first English 'whodunits'. Collins' formula 'Make 'em laugh, make 'em weep, make 'em wait' proved successful and Hardy's *Desperate Remedies* shows his influence.

**Committee-Man of 'The Terror', A.** This slight story, published in *The Illustrated London News*, November 1896 and collected in *A Changed Man* (1913),\* tells of an abortive affair between a French émigré and the man who, as a member of the Committee of Public Safety, had sentenced her family to the guillotine. Its perfunctory quality suggests it was one of the stories written hastily after *Jude*\* 'to fulfil engagements'.

**Comte, Auguste** (1798–1857). A 'positivist' philosopher who rejected any statement which could not be verified by the methods of empirical science. Hardy read Comte sympathetically but questioned his belief in the inevitable rational progress of mankind.

**Constantine, Lady Viviette** (*Two on a Tower*). An aristocrat with a 'warm and affectionate, perhaps slightly voluptuous temperament' who fell in love with a younger man after being abandoned by her husband. She behaved initially like an infatuated girl but her inherent dignity prompted her to heroic self-sacrifice for her lover.

**Convergence of the Twain, The.** On 15 April 1912, the 'unsinkable' British liner *Titanic* struck an iceberg on her maiden voyage to New York and sank rapidly with the loss of 1,500 lives. Nine days later Hardy completed this poem about the disaster. It was first printed in the souvenir programme of the 'Dramatic and Operatic Matinee in Aid of the *Titanic* Disaster Fund' at Covent Garden on 14 May. The poem combines a technological precision with powerful imaginative vision. 'Over mirrors meant / To glass the opulent / The sea-worm crawls – grotesque, slimed, dumb, indifferent'. The Immanent Will determines such sinister convergences.

**Corfe Castle** (Corvsgate Castle). A spectacular ruin rising from a

Corfe Castle.

cleft in the Purbeck Hills to dominate the surrounding landscape;
the castle, after a long and bloody history, was blown up during the
Civil War. In *The Hand of Ethelberta*★ the heroine became so
enchanted by its 'windy corridors, mildewed dungeons, and tribe
of daws peering invidiously upon her from over head, that she
forgot the flight of time'.

**Country Life.** The historical background to the Wessex★ novels –
the era of the Corn Laws, the advent of rural trade unionism, the
depopulation of the countryside – has encouraged some critics to
approach them as social documents ('The subject of *Tess*★ is the
destruction of the peasantry,' Arnold Kettle). Hardy's account of
country life, however, is primarily artistic in intent. There is regret
at the passing of the old rural certainties but an equally strong
awareness that social conditions are *always* changing. If an urban
readership has tended to romanticize rustic life in Wessex, Hardy
himself had no such illusions.

35

An old hurdle maker.

**Crabbe, George** (1754–1832). English poet, born at Aldeburgh, who practised as a doctor before taking Holy Orders in 1781. He was an amateur naturalist able to look at country life with ruthless honesty and precision. In 1904 Hardy attended the 150th anniversary celebrations of Crabbe's birth at Aldeburgh and honoured him as 'an apostle of realism'.★

**Creedle, Robert** (*The Woodlanders*). A relaxed and contented man who worked for Giles Winterborne★ (and his father before him). At Giles's Christmas party he served Grace Melbury★ with the house-speciality, cabbage, and was unperturbed to discover it harboured a dead slug but 'God forbid that a *live* slug should be seed on any plate of victuals that's served by Robert Creedle'.

**Crick, Dairyman** (*Tess of the D'Urbervilles*). Master-dairyman at Talbothays who showed a straightforward but sincere interest in his employees. His interview with Tess before she worked on his farm showed more interest in her as a person than anyone had shown hitherto. He fathered a happy household of maids and men who lived 'above the line at which neediness ends, and below the line at which "convenances" begin to cramp natural feeling'.

**Criticism.** Hardy was always extremely sensitive to criticism. After he had established his reputation with *Far From the Madding Crowd*★ (1874) he was mostly favourably reviewed until *Tess*★ (1871) and *Jude*★ (1895) when critical discussion of his writing became obscured by moral censure and widespread controversy. His financial position enabled him to pursue his love of poetry regardless of critical approval but he never lost his hostility to critical misunderstandings and attacks.

The early phase of Hardy criticism focused on such matters as topography, biography,★ and philosophy.★ Early critical studies by Havelock-Ellis (1883), J. M. Barrie (1889), and Edmund Gosse (1890) were followed by full-length studies by Lionel Johnson (*The Art of Thomas Hardy*, 1894) and Lascelles Abercrombie (*Thomas Hardy: A Critical Study*, 1912) which drew attention to Hardy's rural settings and tragic vision.

The post 1914–18 war period showed a shift towards a more textual approach. Critics identified the modernity of Hardy's vision within traditional forms, the greatness of his poetry, his mastery of language and narrative. Essays in a Hardy Centennial Issue of *Southern Review* (1940) reflected an increasing contribution from America to Hardy studies.

*Thomas Hardy: The Critical Heritage,* edited Cox (1970) surveys Hardy criticism up to 1914. *Lives, Letters, and the Failure of Criticism, 1928–72* by F. R. Southerington (*Agenda*, 1972) examines critical failure to reach any consensus in the 40 years following his death. Recent critical developments are presented in the Thomas Hardy Society's★ annual *Review*, regular publication of Summer School papers in *Thomas Hardy and the Modern World* (1973), *Budmouth Essays on Thomas Hardy* (1976), and *The Thomas Hardy Year Book* (Toucan Press).

**Cuxsom, Mother** (*The Mayor of Casterbridge*). A fat, jovial widow, with no regrets for the loss of her wife-beating husband. One of the best-informed gossips of Casterbridge, she delivered quaint reflections on Susan Henchard's★ death: 'All her shining keys will be took from her, and her cupboards opened; and little things a' didn't wish seen, anybody will see; and her wishes and ways will all be as nothing!'

# D

**Dance.** As a child Hardy danced to conceal his weeping and loved the energetic and passionate country dances continuing long into the night ('With candles lit and partners fit / For night-long revelry'). He enjoyed the more sophisticated London★ balls ('Reminiscences of a Dancing Man') and found the Dorset★ girls at a Weymouth★ quadrille class somewhat heavier on the arm than their London sisters. He noted in *The Life*★ the last time he 'trod a measure' – in 1895 with Mrs (afterwards Lady) Grove and in old age gave the impression of wanting to join in whenever he witnessed dancing. There are key dance scenes in *Under the Greenwood Tree,*★ *The Return of the Native*★ ('To dance with a man is to concentrate a twelvemonth's regulation fire upon him in the fragment of an hour'), *The Mayor of Casterbridge,*★ *The Woodlanders,*★ and *Tess of the D'Urbervilles*★. Tess, in chapter three, 'participated with a certain zest in the dancing; though, being heart-whole as yet, she enjoyed treading a measure for its own sake ...'

An illustration of 'Tess Returning from the Dance' by Sir Hubert von Herkomer, now in the Dorset County Museum.

**Darkling Thrush, The.** This poem was first printed in *The Graphic* on 19 December 1900 entitled 'By The Century's End'. Its 'aged thrush, frail, gaunt and small' defies the desolation of winter with a 'full hearted evensong / Of joy illimited'. Critics dispute the extent of the hope expressed but the image of the gallant and bedraggled thrush flinging his soul upon the growing gloom remains unforgettable. *The Darkling Thrush* has been set to music for violin and orchestra by Robin Milford (1930).

**Darwin, Charles** (1809–82). A reticent Victorian naturalist who hated the furore created by his *Origin of Species* (1859). Hardy was among the earliest admirers of the controversial work and attended Darwin's funeral in Westminster Abbey on 26 April 1882.

**Day, Fancy** (*Under the Greenwood Tree*). A coquettish schoolmistress with dark brown hair who 'appeared to enjoy the most restful ease when she was in gliding motion'. She married Dick Dewy★ but not before she had flirted with Parson Maybold★ ('You praised me and praise is life to me').

**Defoe, Daniel** (1660–1731). The son of a butcher; a hosiery merchant, traveller, dissenter, secret agent imprisoned for a time, versatile author of *Robinson Crusoe* (1719), *Moll Flanders* (1722), *Journal of the Plague Year* (1722). The young Hardy imitated the 'affected simplicity of Defoe's style'.

**Degrees.** Hardy, sensitive about lacking a University education★ (cf. *Jude the Obscure*), was honoured by five honorary degrees from Aberdeen, Cambridge, Oxford, St Andrews, and Bristol, which he received with great pleasure.

**De La Mare, Walter** (1873–1956). Poet, novelist, short-story writer, and anthologist with great insight into the world of childhood. He was a frequent visitor to Max Gate★ during Hardy's final years. In the middle of the night, shortly before he died, Hardy asked for De La Mare's 'The Listeners' to be read aloud to him.

**Derriman, Benjamin** (*The Trumpet-Major*). A Dickensian character who lived alone in a crumbling manor-house obsessively guarding his fortune. He trusted Anne Garland,★ who used to come and read to him, and when he died of a heart attack it was found he had left her nearly all his property.

**Derriman, Festus** (*The Trumpet-Major*). A red-haired, quarrelsome bully, the nephew of Squire Benjamin Derriman,★ whose love for Anne Garland★ was possessive and frenzied ('It was a positive agony to him to be ridiculed by the object of his affections'). His plans were foiled.

**D'Erlanger, Baron Frederick** (1868–1943). A composer, born in

Paris of a German father and an American mother, who became a British subject. D'Erlanger's opera 'Tess'★ was premiered in 1906 at San Carlos, Naples. Hardy attended the English premiere at Covent Garden on 14 July 1909 and enjoyed Destinn's performance as 'a Dorset dairymaid singing her woes in choice Italian'.

**De Stancy, Charlotte** (*A Laodicean*). A gentle woman who lived at Stancy Castle, once owned by her father, but now in the possession of Paula Power★ of whom she was very fond. She had 'a touch of rusticity in her manner, and that forced absence of reserve which seclusion from society lends to young women . . .' She generously sacrificed her own chances of marrying George Somerset and 'chooses to end up in a convent as a gesture to romantically exclusive affection' (Barbara Hardy). Paula Power, sitting by the fire with Somerset, tearfully says, 'How transitory our best emotions are! In talking of myself I am heartlessly forgetting Charlotte, and becoming happy again. I won't be happy to-night for her sake!'

**Desperate Remedies.** This novel was begun at Weymouth★ in the autumn of 1869 after Hardy had been advised by George Meredith,★ reader for Chapman and Hall, to attempt a story with a more complicated plot. Rejected by Alexander Macmillan★ as far too sensational, it was eventually accepted by Tinsley Brothers on condition the author made some alterations and contributed £75 towards production costs. A fair copy of the revised version was made by Miss Emma Lavinia Gifford,★ Hardy's future wife.

*Desperate Remedies* was published anonymously, in three volumes, on 25 March 1871. A review in *The Spectator* called it a desperate remedy for an emaciated purse. After poor sales the novel was remaindered and Hardy received back only £59. 12*s*. 7*d*. of his initial outlay.

This 'novel of ingenuity', Hardy's first published work, is a complicated mystery-thriller in the mode of Wilkie Collins.★ Although the reader may stumble in the dark corridors of a labyrinthine plot, its Gothic★ elements are made credible by a strong sense of place and some striking visual and sound effects. The characters★ derive from the stereotypes of popular fiction but the orphaned heroine, Cytherea Graye,★ is a charming introduction to Hardy's fascinating portraits of women.★ Her innocence and vulnerability attract the conventional Edward Springrove,★ the sinister villain Aeneas Manston,★ and most daringly, the ageing Miss Cytherea Aldclyffe★ (with whom she shares an intense bed scene). The arresting treatment of suppressed sexuality is one of the various indications in *Desperate Remedies*, clearly an apprentice work, of themes given fuller treatment in later novels.★

No MS of the novel survives, Hardy having destroyed it soon after it was written.

**Destiny and A Blue Cloak.** Hardy's first short-story, published in *The New York Times* 4 October 1874. He used material from it in *The Hand of Ethelberta*★ and made no attempt to publish it in England.

**Dewy, Dick** (*Under the Greenwood Tree*). A staunch, diffident young man, son of tranter Reuben, treble-player in the Mellstock Quire. Although no match at first for the flirtatious Fancy Day,★ he wins her in the end.

**Dewy, William** (*Under the Greenwood Tree*). Dick Dewy's★ grandfather, bass-viol player in the Mellstock Quire. One moonlit night returning across the fields from a wedding he was confronted by a bull. He started to play his fiddle and the bull halted momentarily. Remembering the legend of cattle kneeling on Christmas Eve William Dewy boldly struck into a Nativity hymn: the bull knelt down and he escaped unharmed. He lies in Mellstock churchyard 'just between the second yew-tree and the north aisle'.

**Dialect.** Hardy's knowledge and love of Dorset★ dialect – which he regarded as a genuine tongue and not a corruption – informs his sensitivity to language. His preface to *Select Poems of William Barnes*★ laments the 'silent and inevitable effacements, reducing the speech of this country to uniformity'. Replying to criticism in *Athenaem* (1878) of his use of dialect speech in *The Return of the Native*★ Hardy pointed out that his 'dialect' there was only an artistic approximation designed to reveal character and not an attempt at direct transcription.

**Dickens, Charles** (1812–70). Hardy attended a series of dramatic readings given by Dickens at Hanover Square Rooms. Although an early reviewer of *The Trumpet-Major*★ suggested that 'Mr Hardy seems to be in the way to do for rural life what Dickens did for that of the town, Hardy was not influenced by the elder novelist. Whereas Dickens assumes that life in society *can* be lived successfully Hardy disagrees and believes that something is fundamentally wrong with society. Hardy said, in *The Life,*★ that he constitutionally shrank from social climbing and cared for life as an emotion and not a scientific game; although his countless references to at-homes,

# Diction

dinners, theatre parties, with a glittering muster-roll of high-society names, tend to contradict this.

**Diction.** Hardy strove 'to avoid the jewelled line in poetry' (Letter to Gosse, 1918) and intermingled archaic and commonplace words with apparent disregard for stylistic polish. His absolute fidelity to the experience described, the authenticity of his rhythms and turn of phrase ensure that, in effect, his 'awkward' and 'clumsy' diction works.

**Distracted Preacher, The.** In this story Richard Stockdale, a lonely Methodist preacher, lodges with an attractive widow, Lizzy Newbury, who is a member of the local smuggling ring. (Hardy's grandfather had hidden contraband at Higher Bockhampton.) Stockdale's struggle between conscience and desire is told with an astringency that lifts the tale above its simple rusticity. Hardy later regretted the happy ending put in to satisfy the magazine readers (*New Quarterly* and *Harpers*, 1879). It was collected in *Wessex Tales*★ and dramatized by A. H. Evans for the Hardy Players★ in 1911.

**Donn, Arabella** (*Jude the Obscure*). A pig-jobber's daughter, dark-eyed and strong, 'not exactly handsome but capable of passing as such at a little distance'. Her life was a masterpiece of survival. After easily tricking Jude Fawley★ into marriage she left him and emigrated to Australia where she married a Sydney hotel-keeper. She remarried him in England after getting a divorce from Jude. After her second husband died she took advantage of Jude's drunkenness and degradation to remarry *him* in Christminster. After Jude died she was quick to visit a regatta with the amorous quack Vilbert (Jude's likely successor) but she did concede that 'He's a handsome corpse'. 'Arabella is the bad side of the ignorance and pain of the country, just as Tess★ is the good part of rural courage and beauty and naturalness' (Elizabeth Hardwick).

**Dorchester** (Casterbridge). Dorchester in the mid-nineteenth century was a county, assize and garrison town dominated by commerce and the military rather than fashion or the church and encircled by ancient earthworks and Roman ruins. Although the town still witnessed violent demonstrations, hangings and transportations, its expanding trade brought new schools, circulating libraries, bookshops and greater prosperity. On 16 November 1910 Hardy was given the freedom of the borough of Dorchester and described his Casterbridge as 'a place more Dorchester than Dorchester itself'. Today the basic lines of the town, bounded by

Dorchester today from the north.

tree-lined walks and the river Frome, and the view down the High Street from Top o' Town to Grey's Bridge, have changed remarkably little since Hardy's time. Dorchester from a distance still appears as 'compact as a box of dominoes' (*The Mayor of Casterbridge*).

**Dorchester Grammar School Address.** On 21 July 1927 Hardy, 'in fulfilment of a rash promise', made his last public appearance to lay the commemoration stone of Dorchester Grammar School. His nostalgic speech was printed next day in *The Times*.

**Dorset.** A county in south-west England of remarkable variety and beauty. Paul Nash described Dorset as 'a gigantic face composed of massive and unusual features; at once harsh and tender, alarming yet kind, seeming susceptible to moods, but, in secret, overcast by a noble melancholy – or, simply, the burden of its extraordinary inheritance'. The pastoral nature of Dorset and the comparative lack of ploughing have helped to preserve its landscape★ and a strong sense of the past. Many places carry strong associations – the shipwreckings on Chesil beach, the bloody battles at Maiden★ or Corfe★ castles; other places create an atmosphere of tranquillity – Abbotsbury swannery, the strange hills above Bridport,★ the valleys around Cerne Abbas★ with their quiet churches. No other

43

Dorset County Museum

writer in England has been so closely associated with a region as Hardy has with Dorset and in Wessex* he domesticates it without sacrificing its mystery and antiquity.

**Dorset County Museum.** The Dorset County Museum, founded in 1846, belongs to the Dorset Natural History and Archaeological Society which exists to promote an active interest in archaeology,* natural history, geology, local history and the fine arts. The present building in West High Street, Dorchester was erected by public subscription in 1881 and designed by G. R. Crickmay, Hardy's one-time employer. The main Victorian Hall, a fine example of cast-iron work, contains a reconstruction of Hardy's Max Gate study. The museum houses the largest collection in the world of Hardy's manuscripts, books from his library, and some of his personal possessions.

**Dorsetshire Labourer, The.** This substantial essay was printed in *Longman's Magazine*, July 1883. Hardy criticized the tendency to stereotype agricultural labourers as stolid, uncouth, retarded people. 'It is too much to expect them to remain stagnant and old-fashioned for the pleasure of romantic spectators'. Although welcoming the labourer's greater independence and mobility, partly through the efforts of Joseph Arch,* Hardy also laments the irreparable losses resulting from the changes. 'They have lost touch with their environment, and that sense of long local participancy which is one of the pleasures of age'. Some material from the essay was incorporated into *Tess.* *

**Dualism.** Although artistically united, Hardy's work often makes us aware of the conflicting claims of two worlds, past and present, ancient Wessex* and modern London,* a scientific view of life and an emotional experience of it. 'Hearing what one side has to say you are constantly led to the imagination of what the other side must be feeling'. Despite his disclaimers that he merely recorded 'impressions' and sought for no unified philosophy* he did make such an attempt in *The Dynasts* * and certain of his doctrinal formulations (see Immanent Will*). Out of that creative tension flows some of his best work. His awkward fumblings after 'meaning' or philosophy are transformed by his poetic imagination. By a supreme irony one's immediate and final impression of his work is of a straightforward and knowing simplicity even though he was a man

(*Opposite*) Dorset countryside – Colmer's Hill, outside Bridport.

'who used to notice such things' and who wanted to know what lay beneath them.

**Dugdale, Florence.** See Florence Hardy.

**Duke's Reappearance, The.** This traditional story of a visit to Christopher Swetman's house by a fugitive stranger who could have been the Duke of Monmouth was handed down in Hardy's mother's family. It was collected in *A Changed Man* (1913).★

**D'Urberville, Alec** (*Tess of the D'Urbervilles*). A selfish pseudo-aristocrat and libertine, 'with full lips, badly moulded, though red and smooth, above which was a well-groomed moustache with curled points'. He seduced Tess Durbeyfield★ and, after she had escaped from him exerted power over her a second time, and was murdered by her.

**Durbeyfield, Tess** (*Tess of the D'Urbervilles*). A resilient, life-enhancing girl, 'a peasant by position not by nature', whose modest education (Sixth Standard in the National School) carried her beyond the feckless milieu of her parents without preparing her for the harsh modern world outside. She was seduced by Alec D'Urberville★ and then rebuffed by family, church, and society. Her capacity for renewal enabled her to survive great misfortune and

Nastassia Kinski as Tess in Roman Polanski's *Tess*, 1979.

she met and married Angel Clare.★ He too betrayed her and left for vague farming endeavours in Brazil. D'Urberville claimed her again and in desperation she murdered him. After a brief idyllic reunion with Clare, Tess was apprehended at Stonehenge and hanged at Wintoncester but 'her voice will never be forgotten by those who knew her'.

Tess is described and justified by Hardy with an extraordinary passion and intensity. 'This unsophisticated girl, with the round bare arms, the rainy face and hair, the suspended attitude of a friendly leopard at pause', combines, for Hardy, the natural beauty of a peasant-girl with the poise of an aristocrat. She is both simple woman 'leading her own precious life' and universalized figure for all wronged women.

**During Wind and Rain.** One of Hardy's greatest poems and the subject of much critical comment. Scenes from Emma's★ child-hood – musical evenings, summer days in the garden, the upheaval of moving house – are described as though happening in the present; the refrain to each verse laments that they have all, in fact, irrevocably passed. 'Ah, no; the years O! / How the sick leaves reel down in throngs!'

**Dynasts, The.** A unique epic drama of the Napoleonic Wars for which Hardy gathered material for over 20 years. It was published by Macmillan in three parts in 1904, 1906, 1908 and in a single volume in 1910.

Hardy deploys an idiosyncratic mixture of prose, blank verse, song, stage-direction, and dumb-show to re-create the events of history from Trafalgar to Waterloo. His vast panoramic show is observed by spirits 'with the absently critical gaze of villagers promoted to metaphysical status' (John Bayley). The dominance of these 'impersonated abstractions or Intelligences' leads Hardy to question the scope of human freedom. Within this cumbersome and potentially ludicrous form teems a great deal of convincing life. *The Dynasts* has been aptly compared to a film-script. We see armies glide over the earth and then get a sudden close-up of combatants 'discharging musketry in each other's faces'. The historical charac-ters★ seem stiffly fustian relics and then the drama bursts into life with a brilliant dumb-show: 'They begin knocking the furniture to pieces, tearing down the hangings ... In the rout a musical box is swept off a table, and starts playing a serenade as it falls to the floor. The mob desists dubiously and goes out; the musical box upon the floor plays on, the taper burns to its socket, and the room becomes wrapt in the shades of night'.

Max Beerbohn,★ later to write a fine parody of it, observed that 'to say it were easy to ridicule such a work is but a tribute to the sublimity of Mr Hardy's intent, and the newness and strangeness of his means'. *The Dynasts* is now receiving much more critical attention and respect.

Harley Granville-Barker's★ stage production opened in London on 15 November 1914. Radio adaptations were broadcast in 1933, 1940, 1943, 1951, 1967.

# E

**Education.** Hardy was primarily self-taught. His formal education began in 1848 at the village school, Lower Bockhampton, and continued at Isaac Last's non-conformist school in Dorchester★ from 1849–56. While studying architecture★ under John Hicks he taught himself Greek and benefited from some stimulating com-

Victorian reading-room at Puddletown.

panionship, especially from William Barnes★ and Horace Moule.★ He was a voracious reader and note-taker and made regular visits in London to the British Museum★ and the National Gallery. This methodical approach induced in him an abstract and rigid conception of thinking reflected in the suggestion that 'thought is a disease of the flesh' (*The Return of the Native*★). 'The thought, the reasoning that he respected and hated and feared was hatchet-like, reductive, mechanical' (A. J. O. Cockshut).

Hardy's deepest and best knowledge was inherited and tempermental – not acquired: he possessed the knowledge that comes from feeling. His unique experience of both an ancient rural world and a changing modern one was an education in itself but Hardy's knowledge was instinctive and personal.

The year before he died Hardy delivered an address after laying the foundation stone of the New Dorchester Grammar School on 21 July 1927. and praised the headmaster for his modern ideas on education. He also praised the school's pleasant location, 'near enough to the sea to get very distinct whiffs of marine air' and not beyond the walking powers of the smallest boy in the area.

**Egdon Heath.** Hardy's famous creation based on the wild heathlands between Stinsford★ and Wareham.★ Literary pilgrims may be

Labourers on Egdon Heath.

surprised by its comparative smallness but at dusk it still takes on something of the mysterious vastness depicted in *The Return of the Native*,★ a place which 'reduced to insignificance by its seamed and antique features the wildest turmoil of a single man.'

**Eliot, George** (Mary Ann Cross, *nee* Evans, 1819–80). A supremely intelligent writer whose novels, written quite late in her life, celebrate life's humour and pathos and the salutary effects of suffering. Hardy admired her as a thinker but found her country characters 'more like small townsfolk than rustics ... evidencing a woman's wit cast in country dialogue rather than real country humour'.

**Eliot, Thomas Stearns** (1888–1965). Poet, dramatist, and critic, born at St Louis, Missouri, educated at Harvard, the Sorbonne, and Merton College, Oxford, who became a British subject and an Anglican in 1927. His poetry, influenced by the French Symbolists, expresses intense reflections in a classical manner. Eliot, who once

T. S. Eliot and his wife Vivien.

called poetry an 'escape from personality' wrote a celebrated attack on Hardy who, he argued, wrote 'for the sake of self-expression and the self which he had to express does not strike me as ... particularly wholesome or edifying.' Hardy's morbidity★ and the emotionalism of his characters were also criticized. This surprisingly unbalanced judgement from a critic of such eminence was later modified.

**Ellis, Henry Havelock** (1859–1939). A progressive writer, psychologist, and advocate of free love, whose *Studies in the Psychology of Sex* (1897–1910) led to a prosecution. His survey of Hardy's novels (*Westminster Review*, 1883) was the most important article on Hardy before the publication of *Tess*.★ He gives special attention to Hardy's 'instinct-led women★, who form a series which, for subtle simplicity, for a certain fascinating and incalculable vivacity which is half-ethereal and half-homely, can hardly be matched'.

**Enter a Dragoon.** The dragoon of the story, Sergeant-Major John Clark, returns to the wars leaving Selina Paddock to bring up their child. She is about to marry a kindly local man when her former lover, thought dead in the wars, dramatically returns. He dies of a heart attack during the celebration dance and is buried with full military honours. Selina prefers to remain the dragoon's 'widow in the eyes of Heaven' and lovingly tends his grave. One day she meets there a woman with a small boy who identifies herself as 'the only Mrs John Clark, widow of the late Sergeant-Major of Dragoons'. She apologizes for having pulled up the ivy which Selina had reverently planted to mantle the grave, 'but that common sort of ivy is considered a weed in my part of the country'. *Enter a Dragoon* published in *Harper's* in 1900 was collected in *A Changed Man*★ (1913).

**Essays.** Hardy's essays, collected in *Thomas Hardy's Personal Writings*, edited Orel (1967), suggest by their flatness of style★ and extreme literalness that Hardy was not at ease with this literary form.★ There are still many fascinating expressions in them of Hardy's 'idiosyncratic mode of regard'.

**Essays and Reviews.** A symposium on religious subjects published in 1860 which subjected the Bible to modern methods of textual criticism and earned the contributors, Rev. Henry Bristow, Frederick Temple, Mark Pattison, Benjamin Jowett, Rowland Williams, Baden Powell, and C. W. Goodwin, the nickname 'The Seven Against Christ'. Hardy read the essays and discussed them with Horace Moule.★

**Everdene, Bathsheba** (*Far From the Madding Crowd*). A high-spirited girl who inherits a farm which she decides to manage herself. Her effortless beauty ('in her new riding-habit of myrtle-green, which fitted her to the waist as a rind fits its fruit') causes emotional havoc in rural Weatherbury. After rejecting the worthy Gabriel Oak,★ and flirting with the deeply emotional Farmer Boldwood★ she herself falls victim to a physical passion for the glamorous Sergeant Troy.★ (No surprise to the local gossips who knew 'She was going to be a governess, only she was too wild'.) She learns to realize the limitations as well as the strengths of her womanliness, accepts responsibilities towards her farm and those dependent on it, and fittingly marries the patient Oak on a damp, disagreeable morning 'in a cloak that reached her clogs'.

**Evolutionary Meliorism.** Hardy's attempt to formulate a theory for the improvement of mankind. The Immanent Will, the blind force which governs the universe, must become conscious. This might be achieved through the cumulative effect of human beings who *are* consciously increasing their awareness and competence; the individual must search for 'chinks of possibility', become more adaptable, stop relying complacently on 'Providence'. 'Pain to all ... tongued or dumb, shall be kept down to a minimum by loving-kindness, operating through scientific knowledge, and actuated by the modicum of free will conjecturally possessed by organic life.' (Preface to *Late Lyrics and Earlier*, 1922.)

# F

**Faces.** Hardy, who wrote 'I am the family face / Flesh perishes, I live on' ('Heredity'), makes striking use of face–images in his writing. Just as Tolstoy scrutinized people's hands as revelations of character so Hardy studies their faces. In *The Return of the Native*★ Eustacia Vye★ sees behind her Clym Yeobright's 'ashy, haggard, and terrible face' reflected in the mirror as she combs her hair. 'The death-like pallor of his face flew across into hers'.

In the poem 'The Face at the Casement' two lovers pass a house in which the girl's former lover lies dying. A message of cheer is sent in, thanks are returned, the couple drive on. The man, unaccountably, turns his head and 'Pressed against an upper lattice / Was a white face gazing at us'. Yielding to a sudden impulse the man puts his arm around his partner's waist and 'The pale face vanished quick / As if blasted from the casement.'

**Famous Tragedy of the Queen of Cornwall, The.** Hardy's last major creative work was begun in September 1916 after he had revisited Tintagel. Laid aside and not completed until April 1923, it was published by Macmillan on 15 November 1923 and first performed, by the Hardy Players,★ at the Corn Exchange, Dorchester,★ from 28–30 November, and in London the following year.

It is 'a play for mummers, in one act, requiring no theatre or scenery' and tells the story of King Mark, the two Iseults, and Tristan. It preserves unity of time★ and place, uses a classical chorus, and shows Hardy's unique conception of drama. An operatic version by Rutland Boughton was performed in Hardy's presence at the Glastonbury Festival in 1924. The MS is in the Dorset County Museum.★

**Far From the Madding Crowd.** In November 1872 Leslie Stephen,★ impressed with *Under the Greenwood Tree*,★ asked Hardy for a story for *Cornhill Magazine*. The result was Hardy's first major achievement, *Far From the Madding Crowd*, written at Higher Bockhampton★ among the rural scenes and characters★ described.

Room at Higher Bockhampton in which Hardy wrote *Far From the Madding Crowd*.

It was serialized anonymously from January to December 1874 and, wishing 'merely to be considered a good hand at a serial', Hardy was surprised when the reviewer in *The Spectator* attributed the new work to George Eliot.★ The two-volume first edition, with illustrations by Helen Paterson★ was published by Smith, Elder and Co. on 23 November 1874 under the author's name in an edition of 1,000 copies at 21s. It was an immediate success.

The pastoral love story of Bathsheba Everdene and her three suitors, the faithful shepherd Oak,★ the passionate farmer Boldwood,★ and the dashing sergeant Troy★ unfolds spaciously in richly coloured scenes. The lives of the main protagonists cross those of ordinary folk whose cheerful acceptance of their workbound lot places the romantic confusions in perspective. Hardy gently exposes human folly against the timeless rural certainties and *Far From the Madding Crowd* – for all its upsets and disasters, is a great comic novel which Hardy later recognized as containing something 'that I could not have put there if I had been older'. It inaugurates the creation of Wessex,★ Hardy's 'partly real, partly dream country', named here for the first time.

*Far From the Madding Crowd* was dramatized by J. Comyns Carr and seen by Hardy and Emma★ at the Prince of Wales Theatre, Liverpool, in February 1882. The same year a play by Arthur Pinero,★ *The Squire*, based on a plot suggested by his management, was so similar to Hardy's novel that charges of plagiarism were raised.

A film★ version directed by John Schlesinger in 1967 with Julie Christie as Bathsheba Everdene, Alan Bates as Gabriel Oak, Peter Finch as Farmer Boldwood, and Terence Stamp as Sergeant Troy was made on location in Dorset.★

The MS of *Far From the Madding Crowd*, believed lost, was discovered in 1918 and auctioned on 22 April at a Red Cross sale at Christies. It is now the property of Mr Edwin Thorne.

**Farfrae, Donald** (*The Mayor of Casterbridge*). An opportunist Scotsman admired for his forthright, confident manner and his fine renderings of sentimental ballads. He was a successful businessman who approached human relationships in the same efficient way.

**Farfrae (née Newson), Elizabeth-Jane** (*The Mayor of Caster-bridge*). A reflective and subtle-souled girl who patiently educated herself – 'never a gloom in Elizabeth-Jane's soul but she knew well how it came there'. She coped with the death of her mother and the

Elizabeth-Jane (Janet Maw) and Susan Henchard (Anne Stallybrass) in the BBC2 production of *The Mayor of Casterbridge*, 1977.

confusion surrounding the true identity of her father. Her reticence in dress and refusal 'to be too gay on any account' rendered her the more attractive, and she eventually married Donald Farfrae.★ 'As the lively and sparkling emotions of her early married life cohered into an equable serenity, the finer movements of her nature found scope in discovering to the narrow-lived ones around her the secret (as she had once learnt it) of making limited opportunities endurable.'

**Farfrae, Lucetta** (*The Mayor of Casterbridge*). A genteel, nervous woman, haunted by her insecure past, who inherited money and was able to secure a husband in Donald Farfrae.★ The rabble of Casterbridge organized a primitive reminder of her involvement with Michael Henchard★ and she died of shock.

**Fatalism.** The objection to Hardy's fatalism, his stacking the odds against his characters,★ has been eloquently expressed by E. M. Forster★ in *Aspects of the Novel*: 'Hardy arranges his plot with emphasis on causality, the ground plan is a plot, and the characters are altered to acquiesce in its requirements ... They are finally bound hand and foot, there is a ceaseless emphasis on fate ...' It is ironical that Hardy's characters still convey a sense of their own precious individuality and uniqueness within his creaking and doom-ridden plots.

Hardy's 'Fatalism' should also be seen in the context of country life, with its resignation to shared disasters and the rejection of any factitious enthusiasm. 'Well, we hardly know how to look at things in these times!' said Solomon (in *The Mayor of Casterbridge*★). 'There was a man dropped down dead yesterday, not so very many miles from here; and what wi' that, and this moist weather, 'tis scarce worth one's while to begin any work o' consequence today. I'm in such a low key with drinking nothing but small table ninepenny this last week or two that I shall call and warm up at the Mar'ners as I pass along.'

The view that Hardy's attitude to character is *totally* deterministic has been refuted in Roy Morrell's book *Thomas Hardy: The Will and the Way* (1965). Hardy's plots contain possibilities as well as actualities and there are plenty of instances of characters evading choice rather than lacking it.

**Fawley, Jude** (*Jude the Obscure*). A poor orphan who aspires to educate himself and seek a better life. He is tricked into marriage by the coarse Arabella Donn★ and has to sell his books 'to buy saucepans'. His relationship with his cousin, Sue Bridehead,★ whom he sees as 'an anchorage for his thoughts', doesn't live up to his expectations. Jude's anticipation of modern man's attempt to become self-sufficient fails; he experiences terrible sufferings, including the bizarre deaths of his children, and dies cursing the day he was born.

**Fellow Townsmen.** This story opens with a memorable description of Port Bredy (Bridport★), a small town so 'jammed' between steep hills that 'the shepherd on the east hill would shout out lambing intelligence to the shepherd on the west hill over the intervening town chimneys without inconvenience to his voice'. After the prosperous Mr Barnet has consistently failed to win Lucy Savile he finds himself at last in a position to propose marriage to her. She refuses him. Next day she changes her mind but Mr Barnet has left town.

The story, first published in *New Quarterly* and *Harper's* in 1880, was collected in *Wessex Tales* (1888).★ In Dennis Potter's television version in 1973 Jane Asher played Lucy Savile and Kenneth Haigh Mr Barnet.

**Few Crusted Characters, A.** These quintessential Hardy-characters* (including Mr Day, 'the world-ignored local landscape-painter') are prompted to reminiscence in a carrier's van by John Lackland who is returning to his native Longpuddle after 35 years. Christopher Twink, the master-thatcher, recalls the time when the parson refused to marry a drunken Andrey Satchel to Jane Vallens but yielded to her request to lock them in the church till the prospective bridegroom had sobered up. The parson went hunting and forgot his promise. Fortunately the clerk remembered next morning and the couple were duly married and given a hearty breakfast. After many such stories the travellers arrive at Longpuddle. The returning emigrant soon discovers that he is among strangers and unobtrusively leaves. These delightful stories appeared in *Harper's* from March to June 1891 before being collected in *Life's Little Ironies* (1894).*

**Fiddler of the Reels, The.** This story was written for publication in a Chicago World Fair issue of *Scribner's Magazine* in 1893. The fiddler 'Mop' Ollamoor's music bewitches 'young women of fragile and responsive organization' and the efforts of honest Ned Hipcroft to protect his wife Car'line Aspent are powerless before such enchantment. Preternatural elements are disturbingly alive beneath the tale's mundane surface.

**Films.** The first record of a Hardy film is a production of *Tess of the D'Urbervilles** in Autumn 1913 for which no details are given. A film of *Far From the Madding Crowd** was made by Turner films, adapted and directed by Larry Trimble, with Florence Turner as Bathsheba Everdene* and Henry Edwards as Gabriel Oak.* Hardy wrote a synopsis for the trade show and the film was released on 28 February 1916. *The Mayor of Casterbridge** was filmed in 1921, produced by Frank Spring and directed by Sidney Morgan, for Progress Film Co. Fred Groves was Michael Henchard. Hardy watched some of the location filming and drove through Dorchester* with the actors to Maiden Castle.* He was sufficiently impressed with the efforts of these pioneer film-makers to say to Vere H. Collins* 'perhaps the cinematograph will take the place of fiction and novels will die out leaving only poetry'.

A grotesque Hollywood film of *Tess* in modern dress and setting was made in 1924 by Goldwyn with Blanche Sweet as Tess Durbeyfield* and Conrad Nagel as Angel Clare.* A film of *Under the Greenwood Tree** appeared in 1929.

Considering the highly 'cinematic' nature of Hardy's fiction it is

John Schlesinger directing *Far From the Madding Crowd*, 1967.

surprising that no film was made in recent times until John Schlesinger's *Far From the Madding Crowd* (1967) which demonstrated the beautiful visual possibilities of a Hardy film. Roman Polanski's *Tess of the D'Urberville's* (1979), filmed in France, has also shown a great flair for story-telling through images.

**Finzi, Gerald** (1901–56). English composer much inspired by literature. His settings of over 40 Hardy poems, including the collections *Before and After Summer* (1949) and *Earth and Air and Rain* (1936), are distinguished by their reflective lyricism and the subtle relationship between the vocal line and the piano accompaniments.

**Fitzpiers, Dr Edred** (*The Woodlanders*). A young doctor of ancient lineage, a dabbler in science and philosophy,* who regarded his personality 'as one of unbounded possibilities because it was his own'. He pursued his changing desires with more consequences for others than for himself and after a sojourn in the woodlands (during which he acquired a wife) and a trip abroad (with his mistress) he returned to town life unchanged.

**Folklore.** Hardy's writing is steeped in Dorset* folk legends, customs, superstitions, songs, omens, rituals. He acquired his knowledge of folklore through oral tradition and informal observation rather than systematic research and it is integrated into his conception of fiction without becoming intrusive. *Tess*,* for example, is full of folklore: Joan Durbeyfield's 'The Compleat Fortune Teller' (kept safely outside the house); the legend of the D'Urberville coach; the many ill-omens which stalk Tess,* who was herself 'steeped in fancies and prefigurative superstitions'. Conjurers and witches are familiar figures in Wessex* and play a dominant part in such stories as *The Withered Arm*,* *The Mayor of Casterbridge*,* *The Return of the Native*.*

Hardy – who retained at least two superstitions himself: never liking to be touched or to be weighed – deeply regretted the loss of much unwritten folklore as a result of social change. He quoted in his notebooks,* in 1875, Schlegel's view that 'the deepest want and deficiency of modern art lies in the fact that the artists have no mythology'.

**For Conscience' Sake.** This absorbing tale concerns Mr Millborne, a lonely bachelor of means 'whose manner and moods did not excite curiosity or deep friendship'. Twenty years earlier he had deserted a woman and child and now, simply to appease his own conscience, tracks down the wronged woman, marries her, and brings the re-united family to London. Far from bringing happiness to anyone the marriage seems to impede their daughter's prospects of marriage to the Reverend Percival Cope, who suspects the past history of his intended. Moreover, the mother and daughter bitterly resent their uprooting from a successful provincial life in Exonbury where they both taught music.* 'We had society there, people in our own position, who did not expect more of us than we expected of them! Here, where there is so much, there is nothing!' Eventually, Millborne settles them, with ample financial provision, in a charming old manor-house near Ivell (where the Rev. Cope lives) and leaves for the Continent. There he is relieved to read of his daughter's successful marriage to the Rev. Cope but 'his momentary satisfaction was far from being happiness' and he resumes his self-absorbed existence, 'and even when he had been drinking said little'. Hardy shows great insight into Millborne's loneliness and the differences between provincial life and life in the capital. The story was published in *The Fortnightly Review* in March 1891 and collected in *Life's Little Ironies** (1894).

**Ford, Ford Madox** (originally Hueffer) (1873–1939). Novelist, poet, critic, travel-writer, and editor who was generous to other writers throughout his stormy life. He once wrote that Hardy the poet, 'simply takes his lines by the throat and squeezes them until they become as it were mutinously obedient'.

**Form.** Considering the formal limitations imposed by serialization Hardy's novels★ achieve (or stumble upon) an impressive structural variety: somehow each novel finds its appropriate form. The leisurely progress of *Far From the Madding Crowd*,★ culminating in its last-page marriage, contrasts with the 'open' ending of *The Woodlanders*★ where the separate and separated lives are far from resolved. The enclosed, claustrophobic chapters of *The Mayor of Casterbridge*★ marching towards their tragic conclusion, differ from the uneven, shifting phrases of *The Return of the Native*.★ In the latter novel the neat symmetry of the six books is effectively subverted by sudden eruptions of emotional conflict. *Tess of the D'Urbervilles*★ takes the classic form of a pilgrim's progress, inverted in that Tess's★ pilgrimage has no possible goal. The fragmented form of *Jude*,★ the action flung from place to place, seems part of the story of alienation and disintegration. Reviewing the achievement of these novels we can realize that formal freedom – as demanded by his successor D. H. Lawrence★ – would not have suited Hardy who thrived on the tension at play between the demands of a conventional plot and the freedom required for characters★ to be themselves.

**Forster, Edward Morgan** (1879–1970). English novelist, essayist, critic, humanist whose best-known works include *Howard's End* (1910), *A Passage to India* (1924) and *Aspects of the Novel* (1927). Forster made several visits to Max Gate★ and reported finding Hardy a boring conversationalist, especially about books.

On one visit Forster stuck to topics such as the discomfort of charabancs and niceties of grammar until Hardy realized his tactics and 'with commendable pique he insisted on revealing the secrets of his art' (P. N. Furbank's *E. M. Forster: A Life* (1978)).

**Fowles, John** (b. 1926). Novelist living in Lyme Regis whose bestseller *The French Lieutenant's Woman* (1969) declares a debt to Thomas Hardy and places the story in 1867, 'the crucial year of Hardy's own mysterious life'. (In 1867 Hardy returned from London to Dorset and became emotionally involved with his cousin Tryphena Sparks.★)

**Freud, Sigmund** (1856–1939). Whether or not the Austrian

E. M. Forster at Garsington Manor, near Oxford.

psychiatrist's work reached Hardy, it has been used by some of Hardy's critics. In *Thomas Hardy: The Return of the Repressed* (1972), Perry Meisel examines the psychological tensions in Hardy's fiction which are implied but not uttered.

**Friends Beyond.** A beautiful elegy on those buried in Mellstock churchyard with whom, 'at mothy curfew tide', the poet communes. In lines of subtly varying length, the 'friends beyond' ponder without regret the lives they have laid aside. It has been set to music by Hubert James Foss in *Seven Poems of Thomas Hardy* (1925).

# G

**Galsworthy, John** (1867–1933). Novelist and playwright who won the Nobel prize in 1932. His *Forsyte Saga*, which examined the Victorian possessive instinct, has attracted an international audience through a popular television dramatization. Hardy enjoyed

Galsworthy's friendship but considered his characters too materialistic.

**Gardens.** Hardy's birthplace★ had a cottage garden of fruit trees, flowers and vegetables which seemed an extension of the surrounding woods. The house he built at Max Gate★ had a planted Victorian garden, with lawns and flower beds, screened from the outside world by a thick barrier of imported Austrian pines.

Side entrance to the garden at St Juliot rectory, Cornwall.

Hardy's heroines often find themselves in gardens, Elfride Swancourt★ moved anxiously among the dark shrubs and trees of her father's rectory garden to investigate the disturbing sound of a kiss. Anne Garland★ sat demurely in a snug inner garden enclosed by a thorn hedge 'so shapely and dense from incessant clipping that the mill boy could walk along the top without sinking in'. Tess★ moved stealthily as a cat through the rank, unweeded garden of Talbothays 'gathering cuckoo-spittle on her skirts, cracking snails that were underfoot, staining her hands with thistle-milk and slug-slime . . .'

Hardy's affectionate parting from Emma★ under the 'alley of bare boughs overspread' of the wild Victorian garden at St Juliot★ rectory was a turning point in his life. The image of bending boughs shading a lawn recurs strikingly in his poetry.

**Garland, Anne** (*The Trumpet Major*). Hardy's most picturesque heroine who lived with her mother at Overcombe Mill during the exciting years of the Napoleonic Wars and had the attentions of three suitors. The shadow cast over her bright life by 'the stream of recorded history' is conveyed in one of Hardy's most powerful scenes: the passing of *The Victory*, bearing her lover Bob Loveday* to battle and storm, which she watches from the weird landscape of Portland* with a blind old man. She goes home to Overcombe Mill. Her Bob returns in due course and they bid farewell to some friendly departing soldiers, one of whom says to Anne, 'Goodbye! May you remember us as long as it makes 'ee happy, and forget us as soon as it makes 'ee sad'. Hardy reminds us that the battles for which they were leaving told hard on Anne's gallant friends.

**Georgian Poetry.** An early twentieth-century poetic movement which produced five volumes of *Georgian Poetry* between 1911 and 1922. Hardy, something of a father-figure to these young poets, regretted their adoption of such a title (after the reigning monarch) because it confused the poetic chronology. The movement's influence waned when its bucolic verse declined into 'weekend ruralism' and neglected changing post-war sensibilities.

**Gibbon, Edward** (1737–94). A master of English prose whose monumental *Decline and Fall of the Roman Empire* (1776–88) traces the break-up of the ancient world and the establishment of modern civilization. Hardy studied Gibbon's style and always delighted in it. His poem 'Lausanne: In Gibbon's Old Garden' demonstrates how intimately Hardy communes with those writers he admires.

**Gifford, Emma Lavinia.** *See Emma Hardy.*

**Gissing, George Robert** (1857–1903). Novelist whose experiences of poverty and misery are reflected in his work. It is not surprising that after a visit to Max Gate* he deplored Hardy's inclination to fashionable society. 'He is a very difficult man to understand', Gissing wrote to his brother, 'and I suspect that his own home is *not* the best place for getting to know him.'

**Going, The.** The first and, arguably, greatest of *Poems 1912–13.** Hardy laments Emma's* sudden and unexpected death, the estrangement which had blighted their marriage, the impossibility of reparation. The flawless symmetry of the stanzas in no way subdues Hardy's intense emotion; he even rebukes Emma for making him still look for her, 'At the end of the alley of bending boughs / Where so often at dusk you used to be'.

Emma Hardy's favourite walk at Max Gate, the 'alley of bending boughs'.

**Golden Treasury of Songs and Lyrics, The.** An influential nineteenth-century anthology compiled in 1861 by Francis Turner Palgrave (1824–97). Hardy's copy, presented to him by Horace Moule,★ suggests by its markings that he particularly enjoyed the songs and ballads.★

**Gosse, Sir Edmund** (1849–1928). A man of letters whose spiritual autobiography *Father & Son* (1907) describes his revolt against Victorianism. Gosse was Hardy's closest literary friend, wrote perceptively about his work, and asked the celebrated question, 'What has Providence done to Mr Hardy that he should rise up in the arable land of Wessex and shake his fist at his Creator?' (Review of *Jude*★ in *Cosmopolis* 1896).

**Gothic.** Hardy, one-time student and restorer of Gothic architecture,★ formulated a Gothic art-principle based on irregularity, imperfection and surprise. The word 'Gothic' is also applied to a literary genre dealing with horror stories set amidst ruins and haunted castles. *Desperate Remedies*★ has some Gothic elements.

**Granville-Barker, Harley** (1877–1946). Actor, dramatist, director, critic, and author of *Prefaces to Shakespeare* (1927, 1930, 1937, 1945). His production of an abridged *The Dynasts*, with Henry Ainley as 'The Reader', opened at the Kingsway Theatre on 25 November 1914 and ran successfully for 72 performances.

Edmund Gosse with
Hardy at Max Gate.

**Grave by the Handpost, The.** This story tells how one Christmas
night the Chalk-Newton choir witness the unsanctified burial of
Sergeant Holway at a lonely cross roads in Long Ash Lane. He had
killed himself in remorse over his son Luke's unhappy army career.
As the compassionate choirmen 'lift' a carol over the shallow grave
the dead man's son arrives vowing a decent churchyard burial for
his father. A simple headstone is prepared but Luke, suddenly
recalled to active service, is compelled to leave the exhumation and
re-interment to his friends. Time passes and Sergeant Holway
remains in his humble roadside grave. After Waterloo and the
defeat of Napoleon Luke returns and searches the churchyard for
his father's grave. The old rector and many of the choir are dead but
by degrees the truth is learnt. Luke takes his own life in great
anguish leaving word of a wish to be buried at the cross roads beside
his father. 'But the paper was accidentally swept to the floor, and
overlooked till after the funeral, which took place in the ordinary
way in the churchyard.' The story was published in *St James's
Budget* in 1897 and collected in *A Changed Man* (1913).\*

**Graves, Robert** (b. 1895). Poet and novelist whose *Goodbye to All
That* (1929), describing the post-war disillusionment of his genera-

65

tion, mentions conversations with Hardy at Max Gate★ in the 1920s. Hardy once told Graves that he wrote novels★ to a timetable whereas poetry came to him by accident and so he prized it more highly.

**Graye, Cytherea** (*Desperate Remedies*). A girl whose gracefulness of movement 'was fascinating and delightful to an extreme degree'. After the traumatic experience of seeing her father plunge to his death from high scaffolding she faces the further trials of her life with increasing character and understanding ('nobody can enter into another's nature truly, that's what is so grievous').

The freshness of Hardy's first heroine is highlighted by the strange mixture of dull commonplace life and bizarre melodrama which surrounds her. We see her experiencing, on the one hand, a boring train journey, and on the other hand, a terrifying dream in which she is being whipped by Aeneas Manston,★ the novel's villain.

**Great Things.** This poetic celebration of drink, the dance, and love shows no regret for their transience but delight in having experienced such great things. It contrasts with Hardy's grim declaration, in answer to a query, that he had never found alcohol an aid to literary production.

**Greek Tragedy.** Hardy's concept of tragedy, his parallels in *The Return of the Native*★ with structural elements of Greek drama, and allusions★ and references scattered throughout his work to Greek literature evidence his determination to employ his wide knowledge of it although such material is not always integrated convincingly into the narrative.

**Green Slates.** This poem recalls Hardy's visit with Emma★ on 9 March 1870 to Penpethy slate quarries. Fifty years later, green slates on roofs or in passing lorries always seemed to say to him, 'Our home was where you saw her standing in the quarry!'

**Group of Noble Dames, A.** A sequence of ten high-life anecdotes, as told by members of a Wessex★ Antiquarian Club one rainy day, which was published by Osgood McIlvaine on 30 May 1891. These perfunctory and hastily written melodramas (from an author who had just written *Tess of the D'Urbervilles*★) remind us that Hardy's powerful sense of the past is *not* conveyed when he is explicitly presenting historical material. The best story, *Barbara of the House of Grebe*, has horrified some eminent critics but works if read as a fairy-tale rather than as realistic fiction.

# H

**Haggard, Sir Henry Rider** (1856–1925). Author of popular romances including *King Solomon's Mines* (1886) and *Allan Quartermaine* (1887). He was a lifelong farmer and while producing his lengthy report *Rural England* (1902) received a letter from Hardy which regretted that 'village tradition – a vast amount of unwritten folklore,* local chronicle, local topography and nomenclature*' – was being lost as a result of greater mobility among country dwellers.

**Hand, Elizabeth née Swetman** (1778–1837). Hardy's maternal grandmother, 'Betsy', the daughter of a yeoman, was a skilled herbalist, the proud possessor of 30 gowns, and exceptionally well read. She was disinherited after a clandestine marriage in 1804 to a poor servant, Gèorge Hand, who died less than 20 years later leaving her a penniless widow with seven children to be supported by Poor Law relief.

**Hand of Ethelberta, The.** *The Hand of Ethelberta*, begun in Surbiton, was mostly written in Swanage,* and finished in January 1876. It is an ironic comedy of manners in which Hardy surprisingly abandoned the pastoral* mode of his previous success, *Far From the Madding Crowd.**

The heroine, Ethelberta Chickerel,* a butler's daughter, successfully poses as a lady, glitters as a professional story-teller, and, of the four suitors for her hand, eventually marries a dissipated old landowner, Lord Mountclere. She represses her true feelings for the sake of social climbing and wealth.

There are fine passages of natural description, as when Ethelberta runs across a lonely heath to watch a hawk pursuing a wild duck, but Hardy seems ill at ease in the drawing-room and shirks the novel's deeper issues of life as performance, the deracination of metropolitan life, self-alienation.

*The Hand of Ethelberta* was serialized in *Cornhill Magazine* from July 1875 to May 1876, with illustrations by George du Maurier and appeared in America in Sunday issues of the *New York Times*. It first appeared in book form on 3 April 1876 in a two-volume edition published by Smith, Elder.

It did not enjoy the success of its predecessor. D. H. Lawrence* observed that it marks 'the end of the happy endings' with the feeling that 'the best thing to do is kick out the craving for "love" and substitute common sense' (*Study of Thomas Hardy*).

Emma Hardy disliked the novel because there was 'too much about the servants in it'; an unopened copy Hardy had inscribed to her was sold with books from Hardy's library in 1938. The MS has not survived.

**Hardy, Emma Lavinia, née Gifford** (1840–1912). Emma Lavinia Gifford was a solicitor's daughter born in Plymouth★ on 24 November 1840. When she met Hardy in 1870 she was living with her elder sister, the wife of the rector of St Juliot★ in Cornwall. She possessed great vitality, was an accomplished horsewoman and took a childlike delight in nature★ and her modest but not insignificant talents in writing and sketching. She married Hardy on 17 September 1874 at St Peter's Church, Paddington, with her uncle the Reverend Edwin Gifford, Canon of Worcester, officiating. After an initial period of happiness, during which Emma loyally laboured to assist her writer-husband, the marriage★ was poisoned by a tragic 'division'. Emma responded to Hardy's coldness and neglect, his continuing fascination with other women, by turning more to religion. She persevered in attempts to publish her

(*Left*) Portrait of Emma before her marriage (*Right*) Emma in middle-age.

Emma, with Florence Dugdale behind her, on the beach at Worthing
c. 1911.

own work and sought attention through eccentric, even deluded, behaviour. She was outraged by her husband's later thought and writings and the gulf between them was widened still further by her conviction that she had married beneath her. She died a lonely and painful death at Max Gate★ on 27 November 1912.

**Hardy, Florence Emily, née Dugdale** (1879–1937). Florence Dugdale, daughter of a headmaster, was born in Enfield on 12 January 1879. As a shy, introspective teacher and writer of children's books, in her mid-twenties, she was introduced to Hardy and eventually became his secretary and research-assistant. After Emma Hardy's★ death she helped to restore order at Max Gate★ and protect Hardy from unwanted visitors. On 10 February 1914 they were married quietly in Enfield; she was 35, her bridegroom 73. The marriage★ was haunted by Hardy's growing obsession with the memory of his first wife and Florence felt, 'life here is *lonely* beyond words'. She involved herself in Hardy's work (cf. *The*

(*Above left*) Florence and Hardy in the study.

(*Above right*) Florence with the dog 'Wessex'.

(*Left*) Florence after her operation.

*Life*★) but he became increasingly dependent on her and she suffered from bouts of ill-health and depression. She outlived him by only nine years and died on 17 October 1937. (cf. *The Second Mrs Hardy*, Gittings and Manton, 1979.)

**Hardy, Henry** (1851–1928). Hardy's only brother, Henry, was born at Higher Bockhampton★ and continued his father's trade as a builder. He retained his broad Dorset accent, easy-going ways, and natural gaiety and learned to drive a car at the age of 73. Florence Hardy★ described him as 'true, strong and generous in every thought and deed – Giles Winterbourne★ in the flesh'.

Henry Hardy in his motor car, 1922.

**Hardy, Jemima, née Hand** (1813–1904). Hardy's mother, Jemima, had worked as a servant before she married Thomas Hardy, senior★ at Melbury Osmond on 22 December 1839, six months before Hardy was born. She was a person of great dignity who remained young at heart. Her love of books and learning, her rich store of legends and ballads, her fatalistic philosophy★ had a lasting influence on her son. She died on Easter Sunday 1904 and was buried at Stinsford★ in her husband's grave.

Jemima Hardy.

Katherine Hardy.

**Hardy, Katherine** (1856–1940). Hardy's younger sister, Kate, a teacher like her sister Mary,* was a cheerful and resourceful member of the family. Her diary, preserved in the Dorchester County Library, observes how her brother's face, as he lay robed in state for his funeral, had 'the same triumphant look ... that all the others bore – but without the smile'. She died on the hundredth anniversary of her brother's birth.

**Hardy, Mary** (1841–1915). Hardy's favourite sister, Mary, close to him in both age and sympathies, became headmistress of

Mary Hardy.

Dorchester Elementary Girls' school, was a talented painter and church-organist. Her 'remarkably unassertive' character provided ideal companionship for Hardy and they enjoyed country walks together 'shy birds stood watching us, wonder-dumb'. cf. 'Middle-Age Enthusiasms', 'Conjecture', 'Logs on the Hearth', 'Molly Gone', 'Looking Across', 'In the Garden', 'The Sun's Last Look on the Country Girl'.

**Hardy, Mary, née Head** (1772–1857). Hardy's paternal grandmother spent the first 13 years of her orphaned life at Great Fawley.★ During Hardy's childhood she lived at Higher Bockhampton★ and impressed him with her recollections, her knowledge of folklore,★ her descriptions of legendary winters when people had to walk to church along the hedge-tops.

**Hardy Players, The.** An amateur drama group who adopted the title Hardy Players in 1916. They produced dramatized versions of the Wessex novels, by A. H. Evans and, later, T. H. Tilley, which were performed in Dorchester, Weymouth, and London. Hardy supported their work, made suggestions at rehearsals, and provided an adaptation for their culminating triumph – a performance of *Tess*★ in 1924 with Gertrude Bugler★ as Tess.

T. H. Tilley prepares to play Thomas Leaf in *Under the Greenwood Tree* for the Hardy Players in 1910.

**Hardy Society.** It was founded as the Thomas Hardy Festival Society Ltd. in 1968 and became The Thomas Hardy Society in 1973. It promotes the appreciation and study of Hardy through summer schools, lectures, publications, concerts, guided-tours and social events. The society also publishes a quarterly newsletter and an Annual Review and holds International Hardy Summer Schools in Weymouth.

**Hardy, Thomas** (1778–1837). Hardy's grandfather, Thomas, moved into the house at Higher Bockhampton built for him by his father. There he worked as a builder and, according to local legend, part-time smuggler. He was a fine musician and created the celebrated Stinsford* choir. Hardy describes his grandfather's unexpected death in 1837 'inasmuch as he was playing in the church one Sunday, and brought in for burial at the next'.

**Hardy, Thomas** (1811–92). Hardy's father, 'rather amusedly old-fashioned in spite of being decidedly good-looking' was content to remain his entire life at Higher Bockhampton.* He developed his trade as master-mason and builder and was much in demand as a musician, singer and dancer. Hardy admired his father's simple vitality, courtesy, and contentment. He died peacefully in the house in which he was born.

Hardy's father.

**Hardy, Thomas, the author** (1840–1928). Novelist and poet, the
eldest of four children, born in 1840 at Higher Bockhampton of two
strong-charactered families. His mother was a lively-minded
woman ambitious for her son; his father was a master-mason
(whose family had at an earlier time been gentry – according to a
family tradition) who inherited and passed on to his son a passionate
love of music. As a boy he was both highly emotional and intellec-
tually precocious and he regarded this as the clue to his character.
He was of a sombre cast of mind and remained true to his melancholy temperament. He was a born poet who also became a great
novelist. He died at Max Gate★ on 10 January 1928. At the end of his
life he said that given his time over again he would like to have been
an architect in a small country town.

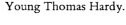

Young Thomas Hardy.

Hardy in middle-age.

The older Hardy.

**Hardy, Sir Thomas Masterman** (1769–1839). A relative of the author; born in Portesham, Dorset,★ and descended (like Hardy himself) from the le Hardys of Jersey. Hardy maintained a life-long interest in his collateral descendant who, as Lord Nelson's flag-captain, survived the battle of Trafalgar (1805). He appears as Captain Hardy in *The Trumpet-Major*★ and *The Dynasts*.★

**Hardy myth.** Like certain other writers (Keats,★ Tennyson,★ Byron★ for example) an exaggerated and caricatured version of Hardy's life and character has established itself over the years. The *Hardy myth* has him as a 'self-taught peasant born in dialect-speaking, rustic cottage setting, who doggedly achieved fame and fortune as a writer of morbid tales. He was mean and miserable . . . etc.' It contains enough truth to survive but not enough to be other than myth.

**Harvest Supper, The.** This ballad★ tells the tale of a maid called Nell, dancing and flirting with a gallant soldier at the harvest-feast, until she fancies she hears the voice of her recently dead lover rebuking her for forgetting him so soon. She resolves neither to dance and sing again nor ever to marry. The poem displays not only Hardy's narrative skill but his ability to evoke a whole scene in a single line such as: 'Red shapes amid the corn'; 'And the parrot, and cage of glittering gold'; 'Your little waist within their hold'; 'There's something outside the wall / That calls me forth to a greening mound'. The poem, dated 'circa 1850' is collected in *Human Shows, Far Phantasies, etc* (1925).

**Hegel, Georg Wilhelm Friedrich** (1770–1831). German philosopher who sought to impose a rational unity on experience through the dialectic of thesis-antithesis-synthesis. Hardy pondered Hegel's thought commenting, '. . . it doesn't help much. These venerable philosophers seem to start wrong; they cannot get away from a prepossession that the world must somehow have been made a comfortable place for man'.

**Henchard, Michael** (*The Mayor of Casterbridge*). A stubborn, intense man, isolated from himself as well as others. In a drunken and quarrelsome mood he sells his wife and child to an itinerant sailor for five guineas. Nearly 20 years later, after rising to become mayor of Casterbridge, his wife returns with her daughter Elizabeth-Jane.★ These, and two other arrivals – Scotsman Donald Farfrae★ and Lucetta,★ Henchard's mistress from long ago – are the catalysts in Henchard's downfall.

His loneliness prompts his fumbling attempts to befriend Farfrae and to win the love and respect of Elizabeth-Jane (who is not, in fact, his daughter). Henchard has an overwhelming need to impose his will on events, to win each self-induced conflict. Towards the end of his story Henchard looks down into the river in which he is about to attempt suicide and he sees an image of himself which had been used in a 'skimmity ride'.

His death achieves a Shakespearian grandeur when, stripped of everything, he dies in the wilds of Wessex★ attended only by the wretched Abel Whittle. As Elizabeth-Jane and Farfrae settle to their comfortable domesticity we remember Henchard for his willingness to accept the dire consequences of his folly. His sufferings were not, he insisted, more than he was able to bear.

**Henniker, Florence** (1855–1923). The daughter of Richard Monckton Milnes, Lord Houghton. When Hardy met her in Dublin in 1893 she was happily married to Lieutenant Arthur Henry Henniker and a well-established society hostess and novelist. Like Hardy she was strongly opposed to cruelty to animals.* Hardy's emotional attachment to this 'charming, intuitive woman' mellowed into a lasting friendship and was the inspiration of several poems, including 'A Broken Appointment' and 'A Thunderstorm in Town'. Hardy's letters to her are published in *One Rare Fair Woman* (edited Hardy & Pinion, 1972).

Florence Henniker.

**Herkomer, Sir Hubert von** (1849–1914). A typical Victorian 'subject' painter who was also a playwright, composer, singer and actor. He became Slade Professor at Oxford in 1899. He painted Hardy's portrait and illustrated some scenes from *Tess** for the serial version. His picture of 'Tess Returning from the Dance' (which Virginia Woolf★ describes as 'an awful engraving') was hung at Max Gate★ and is now in the Dorset County Museum.★

**High-School Lawn, The.** This delightful, impressionist poem captures the gaiety and freshness of high-school girls playing on the lawn one summer afternoon until a bell summons them to class. Beneath the cascade of colour and sound lies an awareness that life is passing swiftly. After they flee to their lessons there is silence. 'So it will be / Some day again / with them – with me.'

**Holst, Gustav** (1874–1934). English composer with an uncompromising directness of utterance. He enjoyed friendship with the older Hardy and wrote, 'Hardy knows my *Planets* because he heard them on a gramophone belonging to T. E. Lawrence★ who was in camp on Egdon heath★ in the Tank Corps!' Just six months before he died Hardy drove with Holst to an Egdon heath radiantly purple with heather and then visited the gallery at Puddletown★ church where some of Hardy's ancestors had sat more than a century earlier. Holst's great tribute to Hardy, the stark orchestral work *Egdon Heath* received its first performance in London in 1928, a month after Hardy's death.

**Homes and Houses.** After their marriage Hardy and his wife took rooms at St David's, Hook Road, Surbiton, and for the next ten years lived in various houses in London, Swanage, Yeovil, Sturminster Newton, Wimbourne Minster and Dorchester. Hardy's family drew attention to their wandering about like tramps. This nomadic pattern is reflected in Hardy's fiction where few of his major characters possess proper homes. cf. *The Homes of Thomas Hardy*, Evelyn Evans (1964). Max Gate,★ a dignified redbrick villa, seemed Hardy's 'house' rather than his 'home'. Many poems explore the distinction. 'The House of Silence' delights in locating its 'poet's bower' in an unromantic urban setting. 'Architectural Masks' contrasts the materialistic dwellers of an old ivied manor-house with the artistic and poetic folk who inhabit a new villa 'in blazing brick and plated show'. Hardy himself felt more at 'home' in the countryside, or musing in Stinsford churchyard, or even patrolling the Esplanade at Weymouth with the Dorset cliffs beyond. At Max Gate he always insisted on accompanying visitors to the end of the drive and Charles Morgan's haunting description in *The Life*★ (p. 402) pictures Hardy standing outside the gate with a lantern swinging in his hand.

The hall and front staircase at Max Gate.

**Honeymoon Time at an Inn.** In this macabre poem an old mirror crashes to the floor of a honeymoon couple's bedroom and lies 'glittering at the pair with a shattered gaze'. Erie lighting effects and foreboding symbolism contribute to the poem's drama. Kenneth Phelps in *The Wormwood Cup* (1975) establishes that the moon's phase while the Hardys were on their honeymoon trip in Rouen was similar to that described in the poem and so this portrait of 'two souls opprest' by sadness and grim portents might have a bio-graphical source.

**Housman, Alfred Edward** (1859–1936). English poet and classical scholar whose pessimism* is mellowed by the grace and beauty of its expression. Hardy first met Housman in 1899 and shows traces of his influence in the war poem 'Drummer Hodge'.

**How I Built Myself a House.** A sketch about the difficulties of building a dream house written, to amuse the pupils of Hardy's employer, Arthur Blomfield.* It was his first published work (*Chamber's Journal*, 1865) and earned him £3. 15s.

**Huett, Izzy** (*Tess of the D'Urbervilles*). A dark-haired dairymaid at Talbothays who fell in love with Angel Clare.* After leaving Tess* he asked Izzy to go to Brazil with him but her insistence that 'nobody could love 'ee more than Tess did!' makes him change his mind and she unselfishly forfeits her own chances. Although a minor character Izzy Huett makes a lasting impression for the warmth and loyalty of her friendship with Tess.

**Human Shows.** Hardy's seventh volume of poetry, the last to appear in his lifetime, was published by Macmillan at 7s. 6d. in an edition of 5,000 on 20 November 1925 and practically sold out on the day of publication. It is a wide-ranging miscellany with many short poems of exceptional quality – such as 'Green Slates',★ 'Ice on the Highway', 'Nobody Comes',★ 'When Oats Were Reaped', 'The High-School Lawn'.★ The volume also reflects Hardy's examination of letters, diaries, and old papers for work on *The Life* in several poems of reminiscence, notably about Emma at St Juliot ('The Frozen Greenhouse') and the death of Horace Moule ('Standing by the Mantelpiece'). The MS is at Yale University Library.

**Humour.** Given his reputation for gloom Hardy's clear-eyed humour surprises in many unexpected ways. It is very English, gentle, and natural and has led John Bayley to suggest that, as with Shakespeare, Hardy's 'natural port was comick'. *The Life* is a veritable anthology of humorous vignettes; the man whose laugh is so

'There might be room for smiles,' Hardy.

loud that it wakes the children asleep three floors above him; the parson whose prayers, in the estimate of a villager, wouldn't save a mouse; the admirer of Hardy's books who had apparently not read any of them. Hardy appreciates the English penchant for grim enjoyment: at the Rabelais Club dinner where 'we were as Rabelaisian as it was possible to be in the foggy circumstances'; a rain-drenched holiday at Weymouth where 'the air will do us good and we can change as soon as we come in'. His humour gains from its reticence and restraint; not for Hardy 'the laceration of laughter at what ceases to amuse' (T. S. Eliot). An essay by F. B. Pinion in *Thomas Hardy:Art and Thought* (1977) has in fact delightfully shown the diversity and range of Hardy's humour.

**Huxley, Thomas Henry** (1825–95). A vigorous free-thinker, supporter of Darwin,* who influenced Victorians by many publications of philosophical and religious subjects and coined the word 'agnostic'* to define his own position. Hardy liked him as a man who united a fearless mind with a warm heart.

**Hymns.** Hymns were familar to Hardy from his childhood at Stinsford, hymn-singing on drowsy summer afternoons (cf. 'Afternoon Service at Mellstock'), to his old age church-going at Holy Trinity Church, Dorchester,* where 'he always seemed very ill at ease and passed his book to his wife for her to find the place'. He is also reputed to have said he liked Holy Trinity Church since they always had his favourite hymn, 'Lead Kindly Light', the reason being that 'when my father spotted him in the congregation he promptly changed the hymns!' (Letter from the rector's daughter to *Sunday Times*, 5 March 1978.)

# I

**Ibsen, Henrik** (1828–1906). Norwegian dramatist whose plays attack conventional hypocrisies which frustrate self-expression. Hardy, an early admirer of Ibsen's plays, deplored the 'blinkered insular taste' which derided them as 'Ibscene', and joined an association for their promotion.

**Imaginative Woman, An.** Ella Marchmill seeks relief from her unhappy marriage by fantasizing a relationship with a poet, Robert Trewe, who previously occupied her seaside lodgings and whom,

Ella Marchmill (Claire Bloom) in the BBC2 *Wessex Tales* production of *An Imaginative Woman*, 1973.

in fact, she never meets. The melodramatic denouement of Trewe's suicide, Ella's death at childbirth, her husband's rejection of the child he mistakenly believes to be Trewe's is offset by the compelling realism with which Hardy describes the progress of Ella Marchmill's fantasy. She illustrates the power of the mind to make its own reality, a central theme in Hardy (cf. Jude Fawley,★ Jocelyn Pierston★).

The story was first printed in *Pall Mall Magazine*, April 1894, added to the 1896 edition of *Wessex Tales*★ and finally, in 1912, included in *Life's Little Ironies.*★

**Immanent Will.** Hardy coined this unwieldy term for his abstract concept of the prime mover of the universe. The Immanent Will is a blind, irresistible, monistic force governing the lives of all men, rulers and servants alike, and which is itself subject to the limitation of being unconscious. Our only hope of improvement is for the Immanent Will to learn from its helpless creation and become conscious. It would then be so appalled at the chaos it has 'willed' that it would either destroy its monstrous universe or 'patiently adjust, amend, and heal' ('The Sleep-Worker'). This philosophical idea was dramatized in *The Dynasts*★ which ends on an up-beat, expressing the hope that deliverance shall be 'offered from the darts that were / Consciousness the Will informing, till it fashion all things fair!'

**Indiscretion in the Life of an Heiress, An.** A much-revised adaptation of Hardy's first, unpublished, novel *The Poor Man and the Lady*. ★ The hero, Egbert Mayne, a young schoolmaster, falls in love with the squire's daughter, Geraldine Allenville, and determines 'to rise to her level by sheer exertion'. The story opens with a beautiful description of an afternoon service at Tollamore church and offers shrewd insights into the effects of social difference on love and culture. It was published in 1878 in *New Quarterly Magazine* and *Harper's Weekly* but Hardy never collected the story and no MS has survived. The story was privately printed by Florence Hardy★ in an edition of 100 copies and was re-issued in 1976.

**Interlopers at the Knap.** One of Hardy's greatest and most characteristic short-stories. It opens with the leisurely pace of a novel as wealthy farmer Charles Darton rides through a gloomy winter evening towards The Knap to marry Sally Hall. Sally's poverty-stricken brother Philip also arrives at that remote place with his wife Helena, whom an astounded Darton recognizes as the girl who had previously rejected him. That evening Philip Hall dies. It seems no surprise when some time later Charles Darton marries Helena instead of Sally. After little more than a year of indifferent marriage Helena also dies. As expected, Darton renews his suit to Sally Hall. That such intricate plotting is contained within the modest confines of a short-story is due to Hardy's brilliant detailing of landscape★ and country-life★ (the custom, for example, of waking the bees by tapping on their hives whenever a death has occurred in the household 'under the belief that if this were not done the bees themselves would pine away and perish during the ensuing year'). Hardy sustains the tension of Darton's renewed suit to Sally but our confident expectations of her eventual acceptance are disturbingly shattered when she adheres to 'her purpose of leading a single life'. Reality intervened and *Interlopers at the Knap* doesn't end like a story. It was first published in *The English Illustrated Magazine* in May 1884 and collected in *Wessex Tales*★ (1888).

**In the Days of Crinoline.** The poem, a high-Victorian anecdote in a stiff and formal style, was entitled 'The Vicar's Young Wife' in the MS and Hardy claimed it was based on a real occurrence.

The crinoline in 1876 as portrayed in *Argosy* magazine.

A vicar, tending his garden, smugly notes his wife's plain tilt bonnet as she sets off for a walk. 'Too dowdy that for coquetries / So I can hoe at ease'. Once out of sight she 'lifts her skirt', unpins an ostrich-feathered hat which she exchanges for the bonnet, and trips off 'in jaunty mood' for an assignation with her lover. The 'crimson-faced sun' observes the couple plunge into a wood untraced. Many hours later the wife, just before returning to her husband, replaces the bonnet. In recompense for such modest attire she receives a fatherly kiss on the cheek.

'In the Days of Crinoline', criticized because 'the situation exists only to demonstrate an ironic point . . . at no time is the poet himself engaged with the subject' (Keith Wilson, *Budmouth Essays*, 1975), does show Hardy's involvement with the paraphernalia of Victorian fashion. This began when, as a small boy, he thrilled to the swish of Julia Augusta Martin's★ heavy silk flounces brushing the font as she entered Stinsford★ church on Sundays.

**Irony.** A rhetorical device which contrasts the literal meaning of an author's words with other possibilities. Hardy's frequent use of irony reflects his temperament and outlook. It enabled him in his novels to circumvent the barriers of Victorian censorship and say, indirectly, 'what everybody nowadays thinks and feels' (Preface to the first edition of *Tess*,★ 1891). In his poetry irony seems a natural mode of utterance. And the supreme irony recoils on Hardy himself. The superb sequence of love poems, *Poems 1912–13*,★ written only after his wife Emma's★ death, radiates a present vitality. 'Beeny Cliff'★ pictures their early excursions on the Cornish coast, 'As we laughed light-heartedly aloft on that clear-sunned March day'. In 'The Haunter' Emma's ghost longs to respond to these tender outpourings. But, 'When I could answer he did not say them: / When I could let him know / How I would like to join in his journeys / Seldom he wished to go'.

**Irving, Sir Henry** (1838–1905). Actor-manager with a mannered style who, with Ellen Terry as his leading-lady, dominated the London stage at the end of the nineteenth century. Hardy, who socialized with Irving, disliked the elaborate staginess of his productions because scenic perfection 'only banished further back the jarring point between illusion and disillusion'.

# J

**James, Henry** (1843–1916). American writer from a rich, gifted family whose highly organized novels contrast European and

Henry James in his study.

American culture and analyse the English character. Hardy criticized James' 'ponderously warm manner of saying nothing in infinite sentences' but valued him as the only contemporary novelist he could read. James was less generous to 'the good little Thomas Hardy' complaining, in a letter to R. L. Stevenson,* that in *Tess** 'the pretence of sexuality is only equalled by the absence of it'. Hardy must have been delighted to inscribe in the margin of the typescript of *The Life** the discovery that James had been rejected by the Rabelais Club in 1879 for the lack of virility in his writing.

**Japanese Thomas Hardy Society.** This society, founded at Nippon University, Tokyo, in 1957, to commemorate the publication of a Hardy bibliography by Mr Hunnosoke Yamamoto, reflects a growing interest in Hardy in Japan. Among the many reasons advanced for this far-flung response to Hardy's work are: his protest against the effects of technological revolution, his keen sense of natural beauty, his microscopic observation, his seasonal awareness, his 'pagan' element, his 'fatalism'.* The Society has published a *Thomas Hardy Glossary* with over 8,000 entries covering dialect,* rare foreign words, neologisms, allusions,* and Wessex* place-names.

**Jefferies, Richard** (1848–87). The son of a Wiltshire farmer who wrote hundreds of articles about the countryside in a poetic and philosophical manner. His novels were less successful because he never fully mastered techniques of plot and characterization. Hardy met him as a young writer and they were linked in the public mind as writers on country matters. There are, however, surprisingly few points of actual contact between them.

**Jude the Obscure.** Hardy's last novel was written at Max Gate* in 1893/4 at a time of worsening relations with his wife Emma.* It is Hardy's most darkly personal creation. A heavily bowdlerized serial version was printed in *Harper's* in London and New York from December 1894, the first instalment entitled 'The Simpleton' and subsequent instalments 'Hearts Insurgent'. The novel, restored to its original form, was published by Osgood, McIlvaine on 1 November 1895 at 6s. and by the following February sales had reached 20,000 despite an unprecedented critical onslaught (which included the Bishop of Wakefield's throwing the book into the fire – as a substitute for the author, Hardy suggested).

Jude Fawley,* an orphan and stonemason with a passion for learning, is diverted from his aspirations by a wretched marriage

Jude Fawley (Robert Powell) and Sue Bridehead (Fiona Walker) in the BBC2 production of *Jude the Obscure*, 1971.

to the vulgar Arabella Donn.★ After she leaves him he goes to Christminster and meets his attractive cousin Sue Bridehead★ for whom he feels an immediate affinity. Their unconventional relationship, strained by Sue's frigidity, her perverse marriage to Jude's old teacher, Richard Phillotson,★ and Jude's lack of success is further tested by the horror of their children's death. (They were hanged by Little Father Time,★ weird son of Jude and Arabella, who then killed himself, leaving the note, 'Done because we are too menny'.) Sue returns to Phillotson and Jude dies in despair.

Hardy's sheer creative force in *Jude* overcomes revulsion at the plot. The characters,★ especially Sue Bridehead, are utterly convincing, their lives increasingly mundane, conditioned by railway★ journeys, domestic proximity, the daily grind, the local pub. We witness the final disintegration of Wessex★ itself and an end to Hardy's novel-writing.

Harry Green's dramatization of *Jude*, produced by Martin Lisemore, with Robert Powell as Jude and Fiona Walker as Sue, was televised by the BBC in 1971.

The MS is in the Fitzwilliam Museum, Cambridge.

**Julie-Jane.** A haunting poem based on Wessex★ folklore★ and custom. Julie-Jane, a 'bubbling and brightsome eyed girl' chooses, on
her death-bed, her coffin bearers from her fancy men. Hardy
marvels at her capacity for joy and laughter in the face of death.

# K

**Keats, John** (1795–1821). Romantic poet whose brief life, revealed
in his letters, was lived for beauty and truth. Hardy's love of Keats
led him to join the National Committee for acquiring Keats's house
(Wentworth Place) as a memorial. He wrote two poems about
Keats, 'At Lulworth Cove a Century Back' and 'At A House in
Hampstead'. Less than three months before he died Hardy spoke in
admiration of the friendship of young Joseph Severn towards
Keats, describing it as 'disinterested' because of Keats' comparative
obscurity. Perhaps Hardy reveals his own loneliness of spirit as he
himself approaches death?

Fair copy of 'At a House in Hampstead' presented by Hardy to Keats'
House, Hampstead.

**Keble, John**

Although Hardy and Keats are both 'romantic' poets, they are, in many ways, antithetical. Keats' philosophy★ of 'negative capability ... the ability to remain in uncertainty and doubt without any irritable reaching after fact and reason' contrasts with Hardy's questing modern consciousness seeking to understand the universe. Keats' 'delicious diligent indolence' contrasts with Hardy's prodigious work-rate.

**Keble, John** (1792–1866). Anglican churchman and scholar whose sermon on *National Apostasy* (1833) inaugurated the Oxford Movement. Hardy admired the unsophisticated devotional verse of Keble's popular *The Christian Year* (1827).

**King's Arms, The.** A hotel, featured in six Hardy novels, situated half-way up Dorchester★ High Street, fronted by a symmetrical early nineteenth-century bay window. The 'Casterbridge Room', where Michael Henchard★ held his banquet, is still used for receptions and wedding-parties.

The King's Arms, Dorchester, today.

**Kingston Maurward** (*Knapwater House*). A substantial Georgian manor house faced in Portland★ stone which towers above woods in the parish of Stinsford.★ Hardy passed it frequently. 'In Her Precincts' recalls his emotional attachment to the lady of the manor, Julia Augusta Martin.★ The poem describes a party at the house: 'The black squares grew to be squares of light / As the eveshade swathed the house and lawn' – but he was an outsider to these refined celebrations. Kingston Maurward is now an agricultural college.

Kingston Maurward.

**Knight, Henry** (*A Pair of Blue Eyes*). A barrister, reviewer, and essayist, in his thirties, whose robust intellect stifled his emotions. Although the heroine saved him from destruction on a cliff-edge by daringly making a rope from her undergarments, his prudishness prevents him from showing his gratitude. The description of Knight's '. . . dark brown hair, curly beard, and crisp moustache: the latter running into the beard on each side of the mouth, and, as usual, hiding the real expression of that organ under a chronic aspect of impassivity' recalls to mind certain photographs of Hardy.

# L

**Landscape.** Landscape in Hardy, rarely mere background, sometimes determines character and sometimes derives added
significance from a scene enacted there. 'Thus Tess★ walks on: a
figure which is part of the landscape' or 'Yet her rainy form is the
Genius still of the spot' ('The Figure in the Scene'). Hardy's sense of
figures in the landscape is perfectly illustrated in Benjamin Stone's
photograph: Lane near Penzance, Cornwall, 1893. The picture
preserves both the temporary moment of the carriage and its
passengers stopping in a Cornish lane and the feeling of auto-
nomous permanence possessed by the tall trees, the tunnelled lane,
the cow in the field. The figures and the landscape are both related
and separate.

This is reflected in John Bayley's description of Hardy's text as
'like a landscape of which the constituent parts – cows, birds, trees,
grass – pay no attention to one another, although they appear as a
total composition to the beholder, the reader' (*An Essay on Hardy*,

'A Lane in Cornwall, 1893' by Sir Benjamin Stone.

1978). Hardy's view that the poetry of a scene varies according to the mind of the perceiver receives confirmation from the antithetical 'readings' of two great critics. D. H. Lawrence★ finds in Hardy's scenery 'a great background, vital and vivid which matters more than the people who move upon it' (*A Study of Thomas Hardy*), whereas for T. S. Eliot★ Hardy's landscape 'is a passive creature which lends itself to an author's mood' (*After Strange Gods*).

**Laodicean, A.** In October 1880, having written 13 chapters of *A Laodicean*, Hardy fell seriously ill and dictated the rest to Emma★ from his sickbed. He said later that fearing it to be his last novel he had put more of his own life into it. Serial publication began in *Harpers* in December 1880. The three-volume English edition of 1,000 copies at 31s. 6d. was published in December 1881 by Sampson Low and Co. and sold poorly.

Paula Power,★ the 'laodicean' heroine, inherits de Stancy castle from her railway-millionaire father and although rich and partially emancipated she remains lukewarm and strangely indifferent. She employs a young architect George Somerset★ who, like Hardy himself, struggles to find the right style★ in life as well as in architecture.★ Their love-story turns to melodrama as the cardboard blackguards of the book, Dare, Havill, and Power, thicken the plot and eventually a sense of fatigue overtakes the proceedings.

There is interest, however, in Hardy's examination of central problems of Victorian culture, 'the incongruities that were daily shaping themselves in the world under the great modern fluctuations of classes and creeds'. A recent interpretation of *A Laodicean* as a feminist novel questions its dubious reputation as Hardy's worst effort. '*A Laodicean* is a feminist novel, and its defects and merits need to be placed in the context of novels about women in the 1870's and 1880's' (Barbara Hardy, introduction to New Wessex Edition, 1975). Paula Power's search for identity and a place in the modern world; some brilliant set-piece descriptions; the abortive baptism, the narrow escape by the railway tunnel, Paula's boudoir or her gymnasium; the force of suppressed emotion often released – yield increasing rewards to readers who have learnt to accommodate Hardy's defects. He himself destroyed the MS.

**Laodiceanism.** Laodiceanism (lukewarmness) was attributed to the church of Laodicea, rebuked for its indifference in Revelations III.15.16. Hardy's 'laodiceanism' was that part of his temperament expressed in his childhood wish not to grow up (*The Life*), his lifelong uncertainty and doubt, suspicion of all forms of dogmatism, and extreme sensitivity to change.

**Larkin, Philip** (b. 1922). English poet born in Coventry who explores the limitations of modern British life without excluding the possibility of humour and love – 'The Less Deceived' (1955), 'The Whitsun Weddings' (1964), 'High Windows' (1974). Larkin has often acknowledged his debt to Hardy and they both share an unsentimental approach to landscape.★

Larkin accepts the industrial landscape's merging of the natural with the artificial, 'Canals with floating of industrial froth ... acres of dismantled cars', in a way that might well have pleased Hardy who, albeit regretfully, accepted the invasion of the railway★ into Wessex★ 'a spot where, by day, a fitful white streak of steam at intervals upon the dark green background denoted intermittent moments of contact between their secluded worlds and modern life' *Tess*★ (Chapter 30).

Larkin's fine critical utterances on Hardy include an influential essay 'Wanted, Good Hardy Critic' (1966).

**Last Signal, The.** As Hardy walked across the fields to the funeral of his friend William Barnes,★ 'something flashed the fire of the sun that was facing it'. It was a reflection from the coffin being carried to the church which Hardy saw as a last signal from his departing friend 'as with a wave of his hand'. The poem employs technical features which Barnes loved to use in his own poems.

**Late Lyrics and Earlier.** Hardy's sixth volume of verse, prefaced with a rather defensive introduction, was published in an edition of 3,500 copies at 7s. 6d. on 23 May 1922 by Macmillan and reprinted twice within a year. Among the representative selection of poems,★ some dating back to the 1860s, are several memorable descriptions of nature's★ seasonal beauty – 'Weathers', 'Summer Schemes', 'A Wet August', 'If It's Ever Spring Again', 'An Autumn Rain-Scene', 'Growth in May'. The last poem 'Surview' is a remarkably frank confession of failure to love. The MSS is in the Dorset County Museum.★

**Lausanne: In Gibbon's Old Garden.** This poem, written on the spot where Edward Gibbon★ completed *The Decline and Fall of the Roman Empire*, incorporates Milton's★ words, 'Truth like a bastard comes into the world' and Gibbon's reflection on the obstacles to truth. It expresses Hardy's conviction that the truth must be told even 'in phrase askance'.

**Lawrence, David Herbert** (1885–1930). English writer, son of a Nottinghamshire miner, whose novels, short-stories, poems, plays, travel-books, criticism, and paintings flow from a creative conflict in him between artist and prophet. His analysis of industrial man's psycho-sexual predicament has greatly influenced twentieth-century literature. Hardy the novelist was Lawrence's true, acknowledged, predecessor ('Where *Jude*★ ends *The Rainbow* begins' (Ian Gregor)). See Lawrence's *Study of Thomas Hardy*.

D. H. Lawrence, 1915.      T. E. Lawrence.

**Lawrence, Thomas Edward** (1888–1935). Individualist who acquired a legendary reputation with the Arab forces during the Great War (*Seven Pillars of Wisdom*, 1926). While stationed in Dorset★ with the Royal Air Force, he visited Hardy at Max Gate★ ('he feels interest in everyone and veneration for no one') and was held in such esteem that he was invited to edit Hardy's diary, i.e. *The Life.*★ T. E. Lawrence has the added distinction of being the only visitor to Max Gate who was not attacked by the notorious dog 'Wessex'.★

**Lea, Hermann** (1869–1952). A versatile farmer, builder, natural historian, photographer and writer who was Hardy's close friend for nearly 30 years and lived at Hardy's home in Higher Bockhampton* from 1913–21. Lea photographed Wessex* places which Hardy helped to identify ('Mr Hardy was in one of his jolliest, most jovial moods'). Both men shared a love of animals* and the closeness of their friendship is revealed in Lea's account, in his reminiscences, of confiding in Hardy an emotional involvement with a much younger woman. Hardy, from a parallel experience in his own life (perhaps Tryphena Sparks*) gave Lea advice which was 'extraordinarily sound, and on some points verging on the prophetic'. Lea's *A Handbook to the Wessex Country of Thomas Hardy* (1904) and *Thomas Hardy's Wessex* (1913) are still invaluable contributions to Hardy topography.

Hermann Lea on his favourite hack at Athelhampton.

**Letters.** The *Collected Letters of Thomas Hardy* are being published in seven volumes by Oxford University Press (edited by Richard L. Purdy and Michael Millgate). Hardy's reticence and the destruction of some personal letters account for their predominantly business tone and comparative disappointment as self-revelation – although the later letters are, apparently, more expansive. The largest collections of MSS in England are at the Dorset County Museum,★ National Library of Scotland, Brotherton Library, Leeds, Eton School Library, Bodleian Library and several private collections.

**Letters on the War.** A pamphlet containing two letters 'Rheims Cathedral' and 'A Reply to Critics' printed in the *Manchester Guardian* in October 1914 and also for private distribution by Clement Shorter.

**Lewis, Cecil Day** (1904–72). A traditional poet, involved for a time with the poets of the thirties, who sought roots in Thomas Hardy whom he described as a man of compassion 'who preserved through journey-work, fame, obloquy, and disillusionment a singular innocence' (Warton Lecture, 1953). C. Day Lewis is buried in Stinsford★ churchyard.

**Life of Thomas Hardy, The.** This unique work, compiled from old letters,★ diaries and notebooks,★ and an important source for Hardy biography,★ has come to be known as *The Life*. Although

Hardy in his study.

nominally attributed to Florence Hardy★ it is actually a disguised autobiography written in the third person by Hardy himself. As Florence completed the typescript the MS was destroyed leaving Hardy to make, in an unfamiliar calligraphic hand, frequent emendations to the account of his life he chose to bequeath to posterity. Typescript passages omitted from *The Life* are printed in an appendix to *The Personal Notebooks of Thomas Hardy*, edited Richard Taylor (1978).

*The Life* first appeared in two parts under Florence Hardy's name: *The Early Life, 1840–91* on 2 November 1928 and *The Later Years, 1892–1928* on 19 April 1930. It was re-issued in one volume in 1962 as *The Life of Thomas Hardy* still preserving the fiction of Florence completed the typescript the MS was destroyed leaving Hardy's life (e.g. the difficulties of his first marriage), passages of social namedropping, uneven style, and unreliability as an objective portrait, *The Life* abounds with intriguing anecdotes, personal reminiscences, and observations on life and art. It is a unique record of Hardy's 'idiosyncratic mode of regard'.

**Life's Little Ironies.** Hardy's third volume of short-stories – *The Son's Veto,*★ *For Conscience' Sake,*★ *A Tragedy of Two Ambitions,*★ *On the Western Circuit,*★ *To Please His Wife,*★ *The Melancholy Hussar,*★ *The Fiddler of the Reels,*★ *A Tradition of 1804,*★ *A Few Crusted Characters*★ – was published in an edition of 2,000 copies at 6s. by Osgood, McIlvaine and Co. on 22 February 1894. The book profited from the success of *Tess*★ and ran through five impressions before the end of May. In his definitive 1912 edition Hardy removed *The Melancholy Hussar* and *A Tradition of 1804* and added *An Imaginative Woman.*★

**Literary Notes of Thomas Hardy.** Commonplace books begun in the mid-1870s containing extracts copied out by Hardy or, sometimes, Emma.★ The two volumes so far published (Goteborg, edited Lennart Bjork) cover many topics: the cost of the Suez Canal; Plato's opinion that 'of all animals the boy is the most unmanageable'; the fact that more people die between three and six a.m. than at any other time; the legend that Albertus Magnus 'on a frosty winter day turned his snow buried garden into a warm garden★ with birds and flowers'.

**Little Father Time** (*Jude the Obscure*). The prematurely aged son of Jude★ and Arabella★ who never had a childhood and bore the cares of the world on his frail shoulders. 'The boy seemed to have begun with the generals of life, and never to have concerned himself with the particulars. To him the houses, the willows, the obscure fields beyond, were apparently regarded not as brick residences, pollards, meadows; but as human dwellings in the abstract, vegetation, and the wide dark world.' His death-wish found a terrible and grotesque fulfilment. Feeling superfluous he hanged Sue Bridehead's* two children and himself leaving the note, 'Done because we are too menny.'

**London.** Hardy first visited London, when he was seven or eight, with his mother *en route* for Hertfordshire. At Swiss Cottage Hardy looked back and noticed London 'creeping towards them across green fields'. Hardy lived in London from 1862 to 1867 and got to know every street and alley west of St Paul's like a born Londoner. He made full use of the artistic and cultural facilities, and even when he had returned to live in Dorset came up to London for the season with unflagging regularity. However, Hardy was a countryman all his life and really felt an outsider in London. It seemed like a vast hotel and he realized early on that one 'must on no account be doing nothing in London'. In *The Life* Hardy had recorded his nightmarish experience while sleeping in London and feeling in close proximity to a monster with four million heads and eight million

Rotten Row, 1904.

Traffic in Fleet Street at the turn of the century.

eyes! He also observed that St Paul's Cathedral had been standing in London a mere two hundred years whereas its Portland★ stone lay in Dorset★ at least two hundred thousand years. Its present façade thrilled all day to street noises but Hardy imagined the stretches of time it had thrilled to the ferocious tides of West Bay slamming against the island.

Hardy's last visit to London was in April 1920 when he and Florence★ stayed at J. M. Barrie's★ flat, near Adelphi Terrace where he had worked as an architect's assistant nearly 60 years before.

**Loneliness.** One of Hardy's best studies of this theme is found in *Far From the Madding Crowd*.★ Gabriel Oak★ slowly discovers an 'increasing void within him'. Bathsheba Everdene★ discovers that Fanny Robin★ has died giving birth to a child fathered by Sergeant Troy,★ Bathsheba's husband. Seized with a longing to 'speak with someone stronger than herself' she wanders outside Oak's cottage. She sees him through the window; he is reading, and later he kneels down to pray. Bathsheba realizes that for the moment she must 'bear it all alone'.

In the penultimate chapter, 'Beauty in Loneliness', Bathsheba is standing outside the church in her black gown after Troy's death

Florence Hardy at Max
Gate.

when she hears the young choristers practising the hymn 'Lead
Kindly Light, amid the encircling gloom'. Their innocence of the
world's sorrows brings tears to her eyes and liberates her from her
isolation. Then 'a form came quietly into the porch, and on seeing
her, first moved as if to retreat, then paused and regarded her'. It
was Gabriel Oak. His embarrassing meeting with her just when he
was on the verge of 'leaving her to fight her battles alone' heralds a
temporary defeat of loneliness.

**Love.** Lovers of Hardy's work may be confounded by the enigma of
his two marriages★ in which love died, his shallow formulation of
love as mere pursuit ('love lives on propinquity and dies of contact'), his romantic expectations of perpetual radiance. Regardless
of such mysteries, Hardy's greatness rests on his understanding and
expression of this theme in his love poetry, his strong views on the
importance of loving kindness ('without charity we be but tinkling
simples' urges Grammar Oliver in *The Woodlanders*), his haunting
accounts of the absence of love, and his exhaustive study of love in
the Wessex novels.

**Loveday, Bob** (*The Trumpet-Major*). A light-hearted sailor susceptible to the first beautiful woman he meets. His early life is a series of
narrow escapes – from marrying Mathilda Johnson, from being
captured by the press-gang, from death at the battle of Trafalgar
(after he had enlisted voluntarily), from a baker's daughter called

Caroline, and eventually from losing Anne Garland.★ He wins her through the noble generosity of his brother John.

**Loveday, John** (*The Trumpet-Major*). A trumpet-major who generously promotes his brother's romance with a girl he loves himself and then departs for battle, and death. 'The candle held by his father shed its waving light upon John's face and uniform as with a farewell smile he turned on the door-stone, backed by the black night; and in a moment he had plunged into the darkness ...'

# M

**Macmillan, Alexander** (1818–96). Co-founder, with his brother Daniel, of Macmillan publishing house to whom Hardy sent his first novel *The Poor Man and the Lady*.★ Although declining to publish it, Alexander Macmillan wrote a helpful evaluation and said, 'If this is your first book I think you should go on'. When the Hardys moved to London★ in 1878 they began a close association with the family. In 1902 Macmillan became Hardy's exclusive publisher.

**Maiden Castle** (*Mai-Dun*). A massive hill-fort one and a half miles

Maiden Castle.

south-west of Dorchester★ originating in Neolithic times which took its present shape of tumultuous three-fold ramparts during the Early Iron Age and Roman periods. Its grim burial remains include a mutilated corpse and a defender's backbone pierced by a Roman arrowhead (cf. p. 12). 'At one's every step forward it rises higher against the south sky, with an obtrusive personality that compels the senses to regard it and consider.' (Tryst at an Ancient Earthwork.★)

**Manston, Aeneas** (*Desperate Remedies*). A bizarre and sensual villain, given to playing the organ 'with full orchestral power' during violent thunderstorms. His manifold crimes (including the murder and interment of his wife) were detected and he hanged himself in prison.

**Marriage.** Thomas Hardy and Emma Lavinia Gifford★ were married on 17 September 1874 at St Peter's Church Paddington. Two of Emma's relatives were there, her uncle Canon Edwin Hamilton Gifford who performed the ceremony and her brother Walter who gave her away, but none of Hardy's. The second witness was the daughter of Hardy's landlady.

Thomas Hardy and Florence Emily Dugdale★ were married on 10 February 1914 at the parish church, Enfield. The couple walked quietly to and from the church. Florence, wearing a dark travelling costume and a heavy felt hat, was given away by her father. The only others present were Florence's youngest sister Marjorie and Hardy's brother Henry.★

**Martin, Julia Augusta** (1810–83). The lady of the manor at Kingston Maurward★ took a special interest in the youthful Hardy who became emotionally attached to her. His attempt to renew their acquaintance later in London★ proved disastrous but they occasionally corresponded and Hardy preserved their letters.

**Masefield, John** (1878–1967). A 'Georgian'★ poet, best known for his narrative verse, who was a friend of Thomas Hardy in his later years. He became poet laureate in 1930.

**Maugham, William Somerset** (1874–1965). A novelist who reacted against all forms of literary artifice to write with clarity and simplicity. His *Cakes and Ale* (1930) satirizes some aspects of Hardy's life and work, particularly the fashionable worship of great writers.

**Maumbury Rings** (The Ring). A Roman amphitheatre on a prehistoric site immediately south of Dorchester★ on the Weymouth★

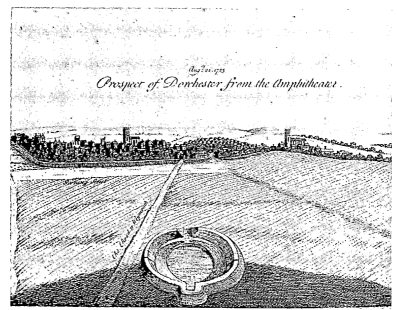

Old print of Maumbury Rings with Dorchester in the background, dated 1723.

road, now enclosed by the railway.★ Hardy's article *Maumbury Ring* (*The Times*, 8 October 1908) describes its bloody history and gives details of recent excavations. Chapter XI of *The Mayor of Casterbridge*★ contains a celebrated description of this melancholy place. 'Some old people said that at certain moments in the summer time, in broad daylight, persons sitting with a book or dozing in the arena had, on lifting their eyes beheld the slopes lined with a gazing legion of Hadrian's soldiery as if watching the gladiatorial combat ...' Here Michael Henchard★ arranges his furtive meeting with Susan,★ the woman he had abandoned 20 years earlier.

**Max Gate.** Hardy's house on the Wareham★ road just outside Dorchester,★ designed by Hardy himself, was finished in June 1885 and named after a neighbouring toll-gate keeper. It is an angular three-storey Victorian villa in red brick surrounded by large grounds thickly planted with trees★ to ensure privacy. Here Hardy wrote *The Woodlanders,*★ *Tess,*★ *Jude,*★ *The Dynasts,*★ and much of his poetry. Max Gate,★ given to the National Trust by Hardy's surviving sister, Kate,★ is now a private residence and not open to the public.

Max Gate.

**Maybold, Parson** (*Under the Greenwood Tree*). A good-looking young vicar of Mellstock with newer ideas than the previous incumbent. His decision to replace the Mellstock Quire with a new-fangled organ was not popular. He proposed to Fancy Day★ who was tempted by his social position but who eventually married Dick Dewy.★

**Mayor of Casterbridge, The.** The novel was written at Shire Hall Place, Dorchester,★ and completed on 17 April 1885. It began its serialization in *The Graphic* on 2 January 1886 and, after consider-able revision, was published in two volumes in an edition of 758 copies at 21s. by Smith, Elder & Co on 10 May 1886. It was well reviewed but 37 copies of the first edition were remaindered. Hardy thought he had spoiled it by cramming too much incident into each chapter but *The Mayor of Casterbridge*, a kind of centre-piece of the Wessex★ novels,★ confirmed his status as a major novelist.

Michael Henchard,★ a hay-trusser in search of work, becomes quarrelsomely drunk and sells his wife and child for five pounds to an itinerant sailor. The plot that follows is Hardy's most elaborate and most successful. The relationships between the six major

Michael Henchard (Alan Bates), taking the road to seek work as a casual labourer in the BBC2 production of *The Mayor of Casterbridge*, 1978.

characters – Henchard, Susan★ his wife, Lucetta★ his one-time mistress, Elizabeth-Jane,★ Susan's daughter by Richard Newson the sailor, Donald Farfrae,★ a Scotsman – become a complex web of lies and deceptions with Henchard's need to impose his will on everyone around him the central catalyst. Not least of the novel's achievements is that although the story 'is more particularly of one man's deeds and character than any other ...' it also presents fascinating portraits of three women★ (especially Elizabeth-Jane), an account of a failed friendship (between Henchard and Farfrae), and an authentic study of a country town in transition. No other Hardy novel conveys the great loneliness★ of spirit felt by those who question life's forms too closely. Henchard had spent 'his life worrying about how to secure his claims to other people and test their claims to him' (Juliet Grindle) and thereby drove them further away. Abel Whittle's loving attention to Henchard in his last hours (returning Henchard's unthinking generosity to his mother in earlier days) shows too late how different his life might have been.

The many dramatizations of *The Mayor of Casterbridge* include: John Drinkwater's 1926 version specially presented in Weymouth★

for Hardy's last visit to the theatre; Howard Rose's radio adaptation in 1928, the first to reach a nationwide audience; Dennis Potter's BBC television dramatization in 1977 with Alan Bates as Michael Henchard.

**Melancholy Hussar of the German Legion, The.** This story is based on an incident, recorded in *The Trumpet-Major Notebook*★ dated 1891, of two German soldiers of the York Hussars shot on Bincombe Down for desertion, 'they dropped instantly, and expired without a groan. The men wheeled in sections, and marched by the bodies in slow time.' It was collected in *Life's Little Ironies* (1894)★ and transferred to *Wessex Tales* (1912).★ Ken Taylor's television dramatization, produced for the BBC 'Wessex Tales' series in 1973 contained some spectacular shots of the execution on the downs.

**Melbury, Grace** (*The Woodlanders*). A reticent country-girl, 'sometimes beautiful at other times not beautiful according to the state of her health and spirits', whose sophisticated education doesn't prevent her ill-advised marriage to Edred Fitzpiers.★ Asked by J. T. Grein for permission to adapt *The Woodlanders* for the theatre

Illustration of Grace Melbury by G. Brownridge.

Hardy pointed out that his implication that the heroine was doomed to an unhappy life with an inconstant husband had to be played down in the book so as not to offend convention.

**Memoranda Notebooks.** *Memoranda I* covers the years 1867–1920 and *Memoranda II* includes entries up to a few months before Hardy's death. The terse entries, often made from earlier notebooks, 'have much to interest the reader alive to the subtleties of Hardy's temperament' (Richard Taylor, *Personal Notebooks of Thomas Hardy, 1978*).

**Men Who March Away.** A patriotic poem about men who fight in the belief that their cause is just. It is dated 5 September 1914. The copyright was not reserved and it was widely reprinted before Hardy collected it in *Moments of Vision* (1917).*

Recruits for the Great War.

**Mere Interlude, A.** The 'mere interlude' of the story comprises astonishing events. Baptista Trewethen, a disillusioned teacher ('I don't care for children – they are unpleasant, troublesome little things . . .') on her way to a marriage of convenience with a rich old man, meets a previous lover and marries him instead. He is soon drowned and she goes ahead with her original marriage plans. Her honeymoon inn had, apparently, been the resting place of her first husband's corpse which has been removed to the room next door.

Thus she spends the night between her two husbands – the living and the dead. Her husband trumps her confession with one of his own: he has four children from a previous marriage and only married her so that she could look after them. In the event, the children forged the link of 'a sterling friendship at least between a pair in whose existence there had threatened to be neither friendship nor love'. This story of almost total plot was first printed in the Bolton Weekly Journal (1885) and then collected in *A Changed Man*★ (1913).

**Meredith, George** (1828–1909). Victorian novelist and poet whose masterpiece, *Modern Love* (1862), a result of nine bad years of marriage with Thomas Love Peacock's daughter, Mary, dismissed by *The Spectator* as 'modern lust', remains surprisingly modern. Hardy, grateful for Meredith's early advice, wrote a poetic tribute 'George Meredith'; 'his words wing on – as live words will'.

**Merrymaking in Question, A.** In this short lyric the joys of music,★ dance,★ and drink are subverted by the ironic images in the second verse of 'a hollow wind, like a bassoon', 'headstones all ranged up as dancers', and 'gargoyles that mouthed to the tune'.

**Mew, Charlotte** (1869–1928). An eccentric poet whose unhappy life ended in suicide. Her talents were recognized by Hardy and Florence★ who entertained her at Max Gate★ in the 1920s.

**Midnight on the Great Western.** In this remarkable poem Hardy describes a forlorn child sitting in a gloomy railway-★ compartment with a ticket stuck in his hat. 'Bewrapt past knowing to what he was going / Or whence he came . . .' The poem's weight of barely controlled emotion has led to speculation about the boy's identity including the extreme suggestion (in *Providence and Mr Hardy*, Deacon and Coleman) that he was a bastard son of Hardy. The boy re-appears as Little Father Time★ in *Jude*.★ *Midnight on the Great Western* has been powerfully set to music by Benjamin Britten★ in *Winter Words* (1954).

**Mill, John Stuart** (1806–73). A practical and creative thinker whose *Autobiography* (1873) describes how he recovered from a precocious education and learnt to think and feel for himself. Hardy, who once heard him speak, admired his personal courage and said he knew *On Liberty* (1859) almost by heart.

**Milton, John** (1608–74). England's great poet, whose seriousness of purpose and grandeur of style★ are seen in *Paradise Lost* (1667), had an unobtrusive but important influence on Hardy. A passage from

'L'Allegro' (1645) with its pastoral★ harmony of work and pleasure, its exquisite colouring ('Of it the earlier season lead / To the tann'd haycock in the mead') suggests the Weatherbury of *Far From the Madding Crowd*.★. The ending of *Tess*,★ 'As soon as they had strength they arose, joined hands again, and went on', recalls the ending of *Paradise Lost*, 'They hand in hand, with wandering steps and slow / Through Eden took their solitary way'. While suffering the outcry over *Jude*★ Hardy took comfort in the fact that Milton had undergone the same indignity at the hands of bigotry and intolerance.

**Mistress of the Farm, The.** J. Comyns Carr's dramatized version of *Far From the Madding Crowd*★ from an earlier dramatization by Hardy. After charges of plagiarism involving Pinero's★ *The Squire*, the play was performed in Liverpool and London in 1882. Hardy dissociated himself from the venture and no complete MSS survives.

**Moments of Vision.** Hardy's fifth and largest volume of verse was published by Macmillan on 30 November 1917. The 159 poems★ are mostly from 1913–16 with only a few re-worked from earlier compositions.

A 'moment of vision' arrives when an incident seems to illuminate whole stretches of experience. In 'The Change', for example, the poet waits at the station among a 'tedious trampling crowd' for the arrival of his beloved. Though travel-tired she greets him affectionately but the meeting provides a vision of love's transience.

Hardy inscribed a copy to Florence Hardy★ with the words '... this first copy of the first edition, to the first of women ...' At his death the MS was given to Magdalen College, Cambridge.

**Monographs.** An invaluable series of 72 essays and recollections of the life, times, and works of Hardy, often by people who knew him personally, published under the general editorship of J. Stevens-Cox by the Toucan Press, St Peter Port, Guernsey. The work has been continued since 1970 in *The Thomas Hardy Year Book*.

**Moore, George** (1852–1933). Anglo-Irish novelist, dramatist, short-story writer whose naturalistic techniques were influenced by Balzac, Zola and Flaubert. *Confessions of a Young Man* (1888) was the first of his vicious criticisms of Hardy which reached a climax in *Conversations in Ebury Street* (1924) which ridiculed Hardy's 'ill-constructed melodramas feebly written in bad grammar'. Hardy retaliated on his death-bed, dictating an 'Epitaph for George

Moore' which ended, 'Heap dustbins on him / They'll not meet / The apex of his self-conceit'. It was the last thing he wrote.

**Morbidity.** Hardy's fascination with gruesome and macabre details makes some parts of *The Life*★ 'an astonishing anthology or necrology of mortuary occasions' (J. I. M. Stewart). He witnessed two hangings, held a candle at an autopsy, contemplated a bridge in Devon from which bastards were drowned, inspected the coffin of someone he had delayed to visit, supervised the removal of jumbled remains from Old St Pancras churchyard. Hardy's rapt contemplation of mortality and decay, his love of churchyards and funerals should be seen in the context of country fatalism★ and his artistic method of intensifying in order to reveal. The morbidity is balanced at times with graveyard humour and the comfort flowing from 'the mood that stillness brings'.

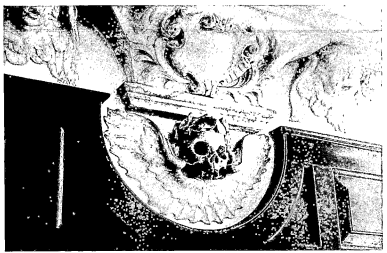

Marble skull in Stinsford church which fascinated Hardy as a boy.

**Morrell, Lady Ottoline** (1872–1938). A distinguished patroness of the arts who sought to live 'on the same plane as poetry and music'.★ At her romantic manor house at Garsington, Oxford, and her London home in Gower Street, she gathered a circle of leading artists and writers of the day including Bertrand Russell, D. H. Lawrence,★ T. S. Eliot,★ W. B. Yeats,★ Lytton Strachey, Virginia Woolf,★ E. M. Forster,★ Siegfried Sassoon★ and many others. She was a keen photographer and 'with a camera held to her

(*Above*) Lady Ottoline Morrell in Venice.

(*Left*) Lady Ottoline Morrell's photograph of Thomas Hardy.

left eye, stalking her subjects' (Julian Morrell Vinogradoff) she captured a unique era in pictures. She provided the model for the character of Hermione Roddice in D. H. Lawrence's *Women in Love.* On 13 August 1925 she made a special visit to Dorset to meet and photograph Thomas Hardy, whose poetry she particularly admired.

**Motoring.** Hardy, sometimes accompanied by Florence★ and 'Wessex',★ went for nostalgic summer trips round Dorset★ in a hired car from 1912 to a year before his death. Harold Voss, his chauffeur, found him an interesting and talkative companion. (*Motoring with Thomas Hardy*, 1962.)

**Moule, Horace Mosley** (1832–73). Fourth son of the Rev. Henry Moule of Fordington, gifted classical scholar, musician, teacher, critic and Hardy's closest friend in early years who guided his reading and encouraged his writing. Moule, brilliant but unstable, abandoned his religious orthodoxy and suffered severe bouts of drunkenness and depression. On 21 September 1873 he killed himself at Cambridge by cutting his throat. Only a few weeks previously Hardy had visited his friend and, on a 'never to be forgotten morning' looked at Ely cathedral glittering above the fens. Hardy's poems about Moule include 'Confession to a Friend in Trouble', 'Standing by the Mantelpiece', 'Before My Friend Arrived'. In the last poem Hardy sits by an eve-lit weir in the Frome meadows looking at Fordington church recalling how many years previously he had sat on the same spot on the eve of Moule's funeral. He seems to take some comfort from the fact that 'The weir still gurgles nigh / The tower is dark on the sky'.

Horace Moule at Fordington vicarage.

**Music.** Hardy was extraordinarily sensitive to music and as a child would dance rapturously to the note of his father's violin (cf. 'The Fiddler of the Reels'★) and be moved to tears by song. His poetry often presents a musical scene: a woman at the piano, a spectral graveside choir, a handcuffed convict bursting into song at a railway-station, the seaside band, afternoon service at Mellstock. It

Puddletown Band c. 1880.

was as a performer that he developed his interest in music, playing the fiddle at country dances. Later, in the setting of Victorian musical evenings at St Juliot,★ he forged an enduring link with Emma.★ 'The Last Performance' gives a poignant account of Emma playing her favourite piano pieces shortly before she died in a forlorn attempt to reawaken Hardy's love for her. He associated orchestral music with his first years in London 'when he was strong and vigorous and enjoyed life immensely'. When he met the composer Grieg he did his best to *talk* about music saying that Wagner's music sounded like the wind and the rain through the trees. Grieg shook his head and said he would rather have the wind and the rain.

# N

**Nature.** Hardy was scornful of a merely scenic or picturesque approach to nature. Thus, 'as Nature was hardly invented at this early point of the century', Bob Loveday's★ Matilda, in *The Trumpet-Major*,★ 'could not say much about the glamour of the hills ...' Hardy said that the 'simply natural' no longer interested him and he turned to the 'much decried, mad, late-Turner rendering' as a more appropriate aesthetic. His descriptions of nature are

The Frome valley in early summer.

often quasi-scientific, striving to break down the surface appearance and look deeper. As Tess★ surveys the Froom valley, 'the ripe hue of the red and dun kine absorbed the evening sunlight, which the white-coated animals returned to the eye in rays almost dazzling ...' His landscapes★ glitter and refract the light, presenting a startling spectacle rather than a restful view. Birds, beasts, insects, flowers, and trees★ are seen differently: the rabbits in *The Return of the Native*★ have the fierce rays of the sun 'blazing through the delicate tissues of each thin-fleshed ear and firing it to a blood-red transparency in which the veins could be seen'; the trees in *A Laodicean* 'were as still as those of a submarine forest'.

**Newman, Cardinal John Henry** (1801–90). Anglican churchman converted to Roman Catholicism in 1845 whose spiritual autobiography *Apologia Pro Vita Sua* (1864) was recommended to Hardy by Horace Moule.★ While praising Newman's style★ Hardy thought that there was 'no first link to his excellent chain of reasoning'. Newman's 'Lead Kindly Light' was one of his favourite hymns.

**Nietzsche, Friedrich Wilhelm** (1844–1900). German philosopher and poet who criticized the complacency of German culture in the age of Bismarck. He rejected Christian morality for which he substituted a doctrine of power calling for the 'revision of all values'. Hardy, whose own pessimism★ was based on a conviction that the universe is flawed, scorned Nietzsche's apparent belief in 'human masterfulness' and perfectibility. J. Hillis Miller observes, in *Distance and Desire* (1970), that 'Hardy's fundamental spiritual movement is the exact opposite of Nietzsche's will to power. It is the will not to will, the will to remain quietly watching on the sidelines.'

**Night in the Old Home.** Hardy, sitting before the fire in his birthplace,* has a vision of his ancestors which makes him envy their ability to 'take of Life what it grants, without question!' The poem has been set to music by Hubert Foss in *Seven Poems By Thomas Hardy* (1925).

**Nobody Comes.** This poem, written on the day Florence Hardy* left a London nursing-home after an operation paints a surrealistic scene of heaving branches outside Max Gate* as Hardy awaits her return. A passing car with glaring headlamps 'whangs along in a world of its own' and nobody comes.

**Nomenclature.** Hardy displays remarkable ingenuity in his choice of names for his characters and the places of Wessex.* His own family-tree was thick with blunt and meaningful names – Childs, Head, Hand, Hardy, Sparks – and he frequently let his characters' names speak for themselves: Paula Power, Gabriel Oak, Sue Bridehead, William Boldwood, Joseph Poorgrass, Little Father Time, Fancy Day. Other names – especially those of the Wessex peasants – come from biblical sources, church history, or Christian tradition: Tess is a diminutive of Theresa, Clym of Clement; St Cleeve of Stephen. Jude recall saints; the inhabitants of Warren's malthouse in *Far From the Madding Crowd,** Jacob, Joseph, Laban and friends are at home with their own poor man's theology and biblical turn of phrase.

When Bathsheba Everdene,* standing by her husband's tomb in Weatherbury churchyard, hears the little voices of the children's choir and is 'stirred by emotions which latterly she had assumed to be altogether dead within her', we see the appropriateness of her being named like the beautiful widow in the Bible.

An article by Casagrande and Lock (Thomas Hardy Society* Review, 1978) shows that Hardy fashioned the name of Michael Henchard* from 'the name of the man who was the Mayor of Dorchester* in 1840 (William Lewis Henning) and the name of a noble Dorchester house (the Trenchard Mansion) that was razed about 1850'.

**Nostalgia.** Hardy's nostalgia is not a sentimental yearning for the good old days but a conviction that the predictable rhythms of rural life, which placed a limit on experience and anticipated disasters as inevitable, are preferable to the deluded Victorian belief in eternal progress.

Children at the village store, Puddletown.

**Notebooks.** The 11 extant notebooks of Thomas Hardy comprise six commonplace books including *The Literary Notebooks*★ and five personal notebooks: *Studies, Specimens 1865* (in the private possession of Richard Purdy); *Memoranda Notebooks I and II;*★ *Schools of Painting Notebook;*★ *The Trumpet-Major Notebook.*★ The last four are published in *The Personal Notebooks of Thomas Hardy* (edited Taylor, Macmillan 1978). The notebooks reflect Hardy's precise working methods, his painstaking eye for detail and his reticence. 'Some men waste their time watching their own existence' (Memoranda I, February 1871).

**Novels.** As time passes the landscape of Hardy's 14 novels takes shape in the mind. The twin peaks of *Tess of the D'Urbervilles*★ and *Jude the Obscure*★ seem the culmination of an artistic journey that began with *Far From the Madding Crowd,*★ Hardy's first and most characteristic masterpiece. *The Mayor of Casterbridge*★ fittingly stands at the centrepoint of Wessex,★ both artistically and topographically, while on either side of it *The Return of the Native*★ and *The Woodlanders*★ achieve their particular greatness without forfeiting idiosyncracies of manner. The eight minor novels create a kaleidoscopic effect with now one, now another coming into focus and perspective. It would be, perhaps, more revealing for a Hardy enthusiast to name his favourite minor novel in any critical debate and the choice would probably be more seasonal than would be the case with the major novels. The present writer would cast his vote for *The Trumpet-Major.*★

**Nunsuch, Susan** (*The Return of the Native*). A 'noisily constructed' woman with clicking pattens and creaking stays who seems a gnarled creature devoid of femininity. She was convinced that Eustacia Vye★ was a witch responsible for casting a spell on her son and she retaliated by jabbing a stocking-needle into Eustacia's arm in church. On the night when Eustacia met her death this sinister figure had made a wax image of her 'enemy', stuck pins into it, and cast it into the fire muttering the Lord's Prayer backwards.

# O

**Oak, Gabriel** (*Far From the Madding Crowd*). A skilful, hardworking shepherd, full of commonsense, and without ambition.

Gabriel Oak (Alan Bates) in the film *Far From the Madding Crowd*.

He was 'only an every-day sort of man' and his 'defects were patent to the blindest'. It was hardly surprising that his blunt proposal to Bathsheba Everdene,* in only the fourth chapter of the novel, should meet with a coquettish refusal. However, Oak's virtues 'were as metals in a mine', he never deserted Bathsheba, and was indeed almost her 'guardian angel'. He also found the time to discover his need for 'a satisfactory form to fill the increasing void within him'. He was rewarded with a quiet but triumphant marriage to Bathsheba. 'Faith', said Coggan ... 'the man hev learnt to say "my wife" in a wonderful naterel way considering how very youthful he is in wedlock as yet....'

**O'Brien, Lady Susan** (1743–1827). A romantic figure in Hardy's imagination. She was the daughter of the first Earl of Ilchester who eloped with a young Drury Lane actor, William O'Brien, and married him to the scandal of all ('Even a footman were preferable', insisted Walpole). After some time in Canada they were able to return and live at Stinsford* House. Hardy's father used to see her, when she was old and lonely, walking in the garden in a red cloak. Hardy venerated her as a kind-hearted and spirited lady, aristocratic but not snobbish.

**Old Mrs Chundle.** This strange story, apparently a true one Hardy heard from Henry Moule, was never printed in Hardy's lifetime. It was published posthumously in 1929 in the *Ladies' Home Journal* (Philadelphia).

The new curate at Kingscreech persuades the deaf old Mrs Chundle to come back to church and fixes a speaking-tube to the pulpit with the lower mouth opposite where she sat. The reek of peppermint, cider, and pickled cabbage which assails the curate from his end of the contraption proves intolerable and the old lady's link with the word of God is summarily removed. A few days later the curate hears that Mrs Chundle is dead – she had strained her heart running uphill to avoid being late for church. In gratitude for the services of her friendly curate Mrs Chundle has left him all she possessed. The curate walks to a lonely spot, kneels down and covers his face, 'a black shape on the hot white of the sunned trackway'.

**On the Western Circuit.** In this story, published in 1891, Edith Harnham, a lonely and unhappily married woman 'whose deeper nature has never been stirred' writes love-letters for her illiterate maid, Anna, to a young barrister who has seduced her. He marries the girl he believed wrote so sensitively and finds himself, like his true correspondent, chained for life to an incompatible partner. Frank Harvey's dramatization, *The Day After The Fair*, ran successfully at the Lyric Theatre in 1972 with Julia Foster as Anna and Deborah Kerr as Edith Harnham.

**Order of Merit.** Hardy, invested with the Order of Merit at Marlborough House on 19 July 1910, said afterwards that he felt he had failed in the accustomed formalities.

**Our Exploits at West Poley.** Hardy's only children's book, a caving adventure, set in the Mendip hills, was rejected by *Youth's Companion* in 1883 and did not find its way into print until ten years later in *The Household* (Boston). It was first published in England in 1952 with an introduction by Richard Purdy.

**Overlooking the River Stour.** Hardy, through the window of his home in Sturminster Newton,★ watches a moor-hen 'planing up shavings of crystal spray' instead of noticing his wife's unhappiness ('the more behind my back'). The mechanical precision of Hardy's observation and description suggest an analogy with Victorian engineering. It has been set to music by Gerald Finzi★ in *Before and After Summer* (1949).

**Owen, Rebekah** (1858–1939). An eccentric, insistent, and proprietorial American admirer of Hardy who crossed the Atlantic in pursuit of her idol and effected an entry into Max Gate★ in 1900. Of her many visits none was more insensitive than one made two days before Emma Hardy's★ death in which Emma, in great pain and near to tears, struggled to entertain her. Rebekah Owen had a lengthy correspondence with Florence Hardy.★ (cf. *Hardy and the Lady from Madison Square* by Carl Weber, 1952.)

**Oxen, The.** This anthology poem, published in *The Times* on 24 December 1915, describes the legend, which Hardy probably heard from his mother, of the oxen kneeling in their stables on Christmas Eve. It expresses Hardy's own wish to believe, 'I should go with him in the gloom / Hoping it might be so'. 'The Oxen' has been often set to music including versions by Gerald Finzi★ (*By Footpath and Stile*, 1925) and C. Armstrong Gibbs (1953).

**Oxford** (Christminster). Although Christminster was a painful symbol in *Jude*★ of exclusivity, Hardy enjoyed his visits to Oxford in his later years especially a memorable visit in June 1923 after his election as Honorary Fellow at Queen's. 'He was obviously happy to be in Oxford, and happy, I think, too, to be of it...' It was the last time Hardy slept away from Max Gate.★

Magdalen Tower and Bridge, Oxford, 1859, by Roger Fenton.

P

**Painters and Painting.** Hardy's fascination for the painter's art, for light and shade, colour, texture, angle and perspective led to a detailed study of painting. In 1865 he began making daily lunchtime visits to the National Gallery where he studied one master per visit for twenty minutes. He executed some good pen and ink sketches himself. He noted in his *Schools of Painting Notebook*★ characteristics of many painters and in his novels alluded to over 60 artists of the Italian, French, Dutch, Spanish, and English schools. ('The reflection from the smooth stagnant surface tinged his face with the greenish shades of Coreggio's nudes.')

Much attention has been paid to Hardy's 'pictorialism', his heightened visual sense, and fondness for grouping figures or 'framing' a scene. Virginia Woolf★ writes in her essay 'The Novels of Thomas Hardy' how 'with a sudden quickening power ... a single scene breaks off from the rest. We see, as if it existed alone and for all time, the waggon with Fanny's dead body inside travelling along the road under the dripping trees ...'

**Pair of Blue Eyes, A.** *A Pair of Blue Eyes*, begun in the summer of 1871 under the title 'A Winning Tongue Had He', was written in London, Cornwall and Dorset during Hardy's courtship of Emma Gifford.★ It contains autobiographical elements, though these should not be exaggerated.

It appeared anonymously in *Tinsley's Magazine* from September 1872 to July 1873 and Hardy provided sketches for some of the illustrations. The novel was published by Tinsley★ Brothers in May 1873 in an edition of 500 copies at 31s. 6d. bearing the author's name for the first time. There was a favourable critical reception but Hardy's publisher disliked it. Hardy himself was attached to it and added stylistic and topographical revisions.

An illustration from *A Pair of Blue Eyes* in the serial version, after a drawing by J. A. Pasquier.

Elfride Swancourt,★ the doomed romantic heroine, 'content to build happiness on any accidental basis that may lie near at hand', seemed gifted with fair prospects. In effect it takes less than five years for death (of a miscarriage only five months after her wedding day) to snatch her from the three men who claimed that they loved her: Stephen Smith,★ a young architect, Henry Knight,★ an older man of letters, Lord Luxellian, the young widower who marries her. The story of Elfride's brief life 'contains many of the impulses and much of the emotion of a tragic ballad'.★ It is clearly the work of a poet and was admired for this reason by Proust,★ Tennyson,★ and Coventry Patmore.★

*A Pair of Blue Eyes* also gains from its precise location by the magnificent Cornish seaboard, that region of 'ghostly birds, the pall-like sea, the frothy wind, the eternal soliloquy of the waters, the bloom of dark purple ...' which gripped Hardy's imagination so permanently. In one of Hardy's greatest scenes Henry Knight faces death literally as he clings to a cliff-edge gazing at the imbedded fossil of a creature with eyes; he feels 'in the presence of a personalized loneliness'.★

The portion of the MS which survives is in the Bliss Collection, New York.

**Pastoral.** A literary genre, based on classical models, depicting the simple, uncorrupted world of shepherds and shepherdesses. Although part of a pastoral tradition reaching back to Spenser and Shakespeare,★ Hardy's arcadia acknowledges the harsh realities of farm-life in nineteenth-century Dorset.★

**Paterson, Helen** (1848–1926). Illustrator of *Far From the Madding*

Helen Paterson.

One of Helen Paterson's illustrations for *Far From the Madding Crowd*.

*Crowd*★ and regarded by Hardy as his best illustrator. She married the poet William Allingham in 1874, the year of Hardy's own marriage, and years later, in the poem 'The Opportunity', Hardy ruefully pondered the brevity of their meeting.

**Patmore, Coventry Kersey Dighton** (1823–96). Minor Victorian poet who celebrated respectable married love in *The Betrothal* (1854), *The Espousals* (1856), *Faithful For Ever* (1860), *The Victories of Love* (1896). He was particularly fond of Hardy's *A Pair of Blue Eyes*★ which he had read to him whenever he was ill.

**Paying Calls.** Only in the last line does the poem reveal that the visited friends are in their graves. Hardy loved visiting the dead and often laid flowers on their graves, and cleared away the moss from the inscriptions. 'Paying Calls' has been set to music by Gerald Finzi★ (*By Footpath and Stile*, 1925).

**Pessimism.** Hardy consistently denied that he was a pessimist. His focus on the darker side of experience was for him a necessary first stage towards a more honest and resourceful life-view. 'If a way to the better there be, it exacts a full look at the worst' ('In Tenebris').

**Perkins, Reverend Thomas.** Hardy's friend, rector of Turnworth from 1893, was, like him, strongly opposed to cruelty to animals.★ He was also a passionate antiquarian and amateur photographer. In 1894 he addressed the Dorset Natural History and Antiquarian

The Reverend
Thomas Perkins.

Field Club in Dorchester 'On the Desirability of a Photographic
Survey of the County' to secure an accurate and permanent record
of the Dorset landscape and its old buildings 'before the touch of the
destroyer came upon them'. He praised Hardy's books as photographs in words 'but I should also like to see photographs in
permanent platinum salts of such men and women as Gabriel Oak★
with his sheep on the Downs, Tranter Dewy with his hogshead of
cider, Old William★ with his bass-viol, pretty fickle Anne Garland★
at the mill, noble John Loveday★ in all his bravery, Old "Sir" John
with his maudlin boasts about his lead-coffined ancestry at Bere
Regis, and poor pure Tess★ among the cows on the dairy farm, or
hacking swedes on the bleak hills of central Dorset'.

**Phantom Horsewoman, The.** The last line of this poem presents
one of Hardy's memorable moments of vision. Emma,★ riding her
horse by the sea at 'a shagged and shaly / Atlantic spot', suddenly
'draws reign and sings to the swing of the tide'. Her stopping,
countered by the eternal movement of the tide surging behind her,
creates a vivid, almost hallucinatory effect which carries the line
beyond the confines of the poem's form. It illustrates the statement,

in *A Pair Of Blue Eyes*,★ 'Every woman who makes a permanent impression on a man is usually recalled to his mind's eye as she appeared in one particular scene'.

**Phillotson, Richard** (*Jude the Obscure*). A shy, generous, middle-aged schoolmaster 'with an unhealthy-looking old-fashioned face' who married Sue Bridehead★ in the hope of appropriating some of her vitality even though she felt a physical aversion for him. After the humiliation of seeing his wife jump out of a window rather than face his advances he agreed to her release even though it cost him his job. When her alternative relationship failed he accepted her back. 'No man ever suffered more inconvenience from his own charity.'

**Philosophy.** Hardy combined a tendency to generalize, to search for the deeper underlying meaning of experience, with an equally strong tendency to see each case as particular and unique. His 'philosophy' was a matter of temperament rather than of systematic thought. He described his novels★ as impressions rather than arguments and objected to attempts to extract a consistent philosophy or world-view from them. There is something old-fashioned and provincial in Hardy's attitude to thought and it is significant that his rural philosophers (cf. Joseph Poorgrass★) seem more at home in Wessex★ than his advanced thinkers (cf. Edred Fitzpiers★).

**Photography.** Hardy's literary career coincided with the invention of photography and reflects this coincidence. Jude,★ who sees in a junk shop a framed photograph of himself which Arabella★ had discarded, falls in love with Sue Bridehead's★ photograph before meeting the girl herself. This primitive confusion of persons and things is a basic ingredient of Hardy's art. It suggests that 'Photographs do not seem to be statements about the world so much as pieces of it' (Susan Sontag, *On Photography*, 1978). In the poem, 'The Photograph', a portrait, of obvious emotional significance, is thrown into the fire. The flames 'gnawed at the delicate bosom's defenceless round' with such apparent realism that the poet averts his eyes at this terrible inversion of developing a photograph.

As with all new inventions Hardy was one of the first to accept and make use of it. A fine poem by Molly Holden, 'T.H.' is based on two well-known photographs of Hardy – one with his bicycle, the other a studio-pose.

**Pierston, Jocelyn** (*The Well-Beloved*). A young sculptor obsessed by ideal beauty who pursues his 'well-beloved' through three generations of one family.

(*Above*) Study of youth and age by Hermann Lea. (*Below*) Hardy has his photograph taken.

**Pinero, Arthur Wing** (1855–1934). The son of a solicitor who went on the stage at 19 and began writing his own plays. His numerous works include *The Magistrate* (1885), *Dandy Dick* (1887), *The Second Mrs Tanqueray* (1893), *Trelawny of the Wells* (1898). His play *The Squire* (1881) bore such similarities to *Far From the Madding Crowd* that it was thought at first to be a plagiarism. It turned out that Pinero had merely made use of ideas given to him by his manager.

**Plymouth.** Important Devonshire seaport since the thirteenth century, much rebuilt after war-time bombings and still an important city in the West Country. Emma Hardy★ spent a happy childhood in Plymouth and Hardy regretted that he never took her to revisit it. Geoffrey Grigson, revisiting the 'marble-paved sea-perfumed town', in the poem 'Hardy's Plymouth', found it 'like the middle-class family of that / Girl you married, much run down'.

**Poems.** The New Wessex★ edition of Hardy's *Complete Poems* (edited by James Gibson) contains 947 poems. Some readers regard Hardy's poetry as a composite achievement which has a greatness beyond the sum of its parts; others see the *Complete Poems* as a treasure chest crammed with individual poems that continue to surprise. Hardy devoted his life until a few months before his death to the writing of poems and revising old ones.

**Poems about Hardy.** Poems about Hardy include: 'Max Gate' by Siegfried Sassoon,★ 'A Luncheon' by Max Beerbohm,★ 'The Heart of Thomas Hardy' by John Betjeman,★ 'In Memoriam Thomas Hardy' by Charles Tomlinson, 'At Thomas Hardy's Birthplace, 1935' by James Wright, 'T.H.' by Molly Holden, 'Hardy's Plymouth' by Geoffrey Grigson.

**Poems of 1912–13.** Twenty-one love poems written after Emma Hardy's★ sudden death on 27 November 1912. 'As expressions of love,★ regret, tenderness, need, they are fit to stand beside Shakespeare's★ sonnets' (John Wain). Emma inhabits these poems with a marvellous vitality – 'bright hatted and gloved', or with 'a wind-tugged tress' flapping against her cheek, or impulsively going up to town without saying goodbye. Though so personal the poems universalize Hardy's experience and are fully accessible to readers who know nothing of Hardy's biography.★

In one of the sequence's greatest poems, 'After a Journey', Hardy describes the countryside around Boscastle★ and St Juliot★ and the

Painting entitled 'Our days were a joy and our path through flowers' by David Inshaw.

girl he met there. The last line, 'Our days were a joy, and our path through flowers', though in the past tense, seems an affirmation of *present* happiness, and part of the peace conveyed in a previous line, 'The waked birds preen and the seals flop lazily'. Another important journey with which the poem is concerned is neither their old excursions together in the past, nor Hardy's mental excursion back to those days, but Emma's journey forward into another life. ('That undiscovered country,' of *Hamlet*, 'from whose bourn no traveller ere returns.') It is her journey into *eternity* that the title also refers to. The poems were published in Satires of Circumstance★ (1914).

**Poems of the Past and the Present.** Hardy's second volume of verse was published by Harper Brothers in November 1901 and was an immediate success confirming Hardy's acceptance as a poet. 'War Poems' describes the sad parting and lonely deaths of the Boer War; 'Poems of Pilgrimage' come from Hardy's visits to Italy in 1887 and Switzerland in 1897 to see the graves of Keats★ and Shelley,★ Edward Gibbon's★ old garden, the ruins of pagan Rome;★ 'In Tenebris' expresses a bitter unhappiness. The MS is in the Bodleian Library, Oxford.

**Poor Man and the Lady, The.** Hardy's first novel, begun in the summer of 1867, was so satirical of high-society, the Church, Victorian institutions, that it was rejected by Macmillan. Chapman and Hall advised toning down the satire and Tinsley's terms were beyond Hardy's means. Hardy eventually adapted it for *An Indiscretion in the Life of an Heiress*,★ and used parts of it in *Under the Greenwood Tree*,★ *Desperate Remedies*★ and *A Pair of Blue Eyes*.★ It is a reflection of Hardy's bitterness against the deeply entrenched class-system in Victorian England that his first novel should have been such a fierce attack upon privilege.

**Poorgrass, Joseph** (*Far From the Madding Crowd*). A bashful rural philosopher who blushed at the sight of Bathsheba Everdene's★ beauty. He considered food and drink 'the gospel of the body, without which we perish, so to speak'. When he was driving the carriage bearing Fanny Robin's★ coffin from Casterbridge to Weatherbury he dropped in at the Buck's Head for a mug of ale and was soon seized with a case of 'the multiplying eye' that prevented him delivering his burden on time. He has the last word in the novel, commenting on the marriage between Gabriel Oak★ and Bathsheba Everdene,★ 'But since 'tis as 'tis, why, it might have been worse, and I feel my thanks accordingly'.

**Portland** (Isle of Slingers). A massive single block of limestone, $4\frac{1}{2}$ miles long by $1\frac{1}{2}$ miles wide, rising at one point to 500 feet. It stretches out 'like the head of a bird in the English channel ... connected with the mainland by a long thin neck of pebbles cast up by the rages of the sea' (*The Well-Beloved★*). It is a place apart (until

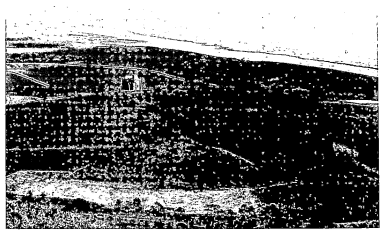

Portland from the hills above Abbotsbury.

Hardy's drawing of The Ridgeway between Dorchester and Weymouth looking towards Portland.

comparatively recently only accessible by ferry), distinctive in customs and beliefs, with a history of defence against the sea and man, of smuggling and shipwreck. The inhabitants were adept with the sling, for which Chesil Bank provided the ammunition.

Portland's stone quarries have supplied material for many of England's greatest buildings. In the last years of his life Hardy formed the habit of watching the passing trains laden with Portland stone. He expressed a fear that the shape of the island would be irrevocably damaged.

**Pound, Ezra** (1885–1972). Influential American poet, translator, critic, and journalist, co-founder of the Imagist movement, tirelessly experimental, who championed the work of new writers including T. S. Eliot★ and James Joyce. He corresponded with Hardy in the 1920s and acknowledged his indebtedness to the clarity of Hardy's poems, 'their complete absorption in their subject'.

**Power, Paula** (*A Laodicean*). An independent heiress who dabbles in physical culture and avant-garde literature but finds her modern life-style superficial and incapable of liberating her from the constraints of Victorian society. She anticipates Sue Bridehead.★

**Powys, John Cowper** (1872–1963). Novelist, poet, and autobiographer whose expansive writings express an individualistic philosophy, and interpret life through ancient myths. He lived for a while in Dorchester★ and some of his novels are set in Hardy country. His two brothers, Theodore Francis (1875–1953) and Llewelyn (1884–1939) were also prolific writers.

**Prefaces.** Hardy's prefaces were mostly written for the uniform Wessex★ Editions in 1895–6 and 1912–13. They give details of composition, topographical information, retrospective reflections, and somewhat defensive reactions to the criticisms of his treatment of marriage in the last three novels. They are collected in *Hardy's Personal Writings* (edited Orel, 1967) along with the eight prefaces Hardy wrote to the works of other writers. Other essays and articles concern literary matters, reminiscences and personal views.

**Private Man on Public Men, A.** This stately poem contrasts noisy competitive city life with the poet's obscure yet contented existence in the country, 'Tasting years of moderate gladness / Mellowed by sundry days of sadness'. It was published posthumously in the *Daily Telegraph* on 26 March 1928.

**Procter, Anne** (1799–1888). The widow of poet Bryan Waller

Procter ('Barry Cornwall'). Her living memories of great literary figures, including Wordsworth, Leigh Hunt, Charles Lamb and John Keats ('a youth whom nobody noticed much'), were of exceptional interest to Hardy. She introduced him to Tennyson and Browning and wrote some delightful comments on his novels.

**Profitable Reading of Fiction, The.** This essay, published in *The Forum*, New York, March 1888, argues that the beneficial 'shifting of the mental perspective into a fictitious world' depends as much on the reader's perspicuity as the novelist's skill. Fiction offers not only narrative excitement but, to active and undulled spirits, intellectual and moral profit.

**Proust, Marcel** (1871–1922). French novelist whose masterpiece of the modern imagination *Remembrance of Things Past (A La Recherche Du Temps Perdu)* was written in the seclusion of his Paris apartment and published between 1913 and 1927 in seven volumes. Proust, who spoke (through his narrator) of finding 'not oneself but a succession of selves', greatly admired Hardy's novels, especially *The Well-Beloved.** Hardy, in turn, acknowledged Proust's achievement in developing still further 'the theory exhibited in *The Well-Beloved*'.

Marcel Proust.

**Puddletown (Weatherbury).** A village on the London road six miles east of Dorchester. Its grey Victorian outskirts enclose well-kept houses and gardens of earlier periods and a beautiful fifteenth-century church with box pews, canopied pulpit, and gallery. Many of Hardy's relatives, including Tryphena Sparks,* lived here and as a child he often walked across the heath to visit them.

# Q

**Quid Hic Agis?** This poem, printed in the *Spectator* in 1916, shows Hardy's susceptibility to memory and association. When he attended Stinsford* church regularly, murmuring 'thanks and praise / In the ancient ways', the scripture readings seemed remote from his own experience. The chapter from Kings was read out each harvest-time, but it was only when Hardy, in old age, felt himself like a prophet in the wilderness that the personal significance of the text broke through to him.

# R

**Railways.** The railway came to Dorchester* on 1 June 1847, when Hardy was seven, and the following year he travelled to London by train with his mother. As a young architect he supervised the removal of skeletons when the Midland Railway made a cutting through Old St Pancras churchyard. His momentous meeting with Emma* in 1870 came after a zig-zag train journey from Dorset to Cornwall 'like a chess knight's move'. His fiction is similarly threaded with railway scenes, especially in *Desperate Remedies,* A Pair of Blue Eyes,* A Laodicean,* and Jude the Obscure.* Some poems set romantic meetings or partings at railway stations. Hardy's most poignant passenger is Ella Marchmill in the short-story, *An Imaginative Woman.* 'The dreary, dreary train; the sun shining in moted beams upon the hot cushions; the dusty permanent way; the mean rows of wire – these things were her accompaniment: while out of the window the deep sea-levels disappeared from her gaze, and with them her poet's home. Heavy-hearted she tried to read, and wept instead.'

Victorian train used in the film *The First Great Train Robbery*.

**Realism.** An artistic attempt to record the details of actual life. Hardy was not, in this sense, a realist. He regarded art as a 'disproportioning of realities, to show more clearly the features that matter in those realities'. He wrote within the conventions of nineteenth-century realism but instinctively reached towards more expressionistic techniques.

**Religion.** 'I have been looking for God 50 years,' Hardy wrote in 1890, 'and I think that if he existed I should have discovered him.' Although not a believer, Hardy wrote about God with a blunt familiarity. cf. 'God's Education', 'God's Funeral' or 'Fragment' in which a group of disgruntled souls waits patiently for God 'to know things that have been going on earth...' He reached a late conviction that poetry and religion touched each other, 'are, indeed often but different names for the same thing – these, I say, the visible signs of mental and emotional life, must like all other things keep moving, becoming ...' (Preface to *'Late Lyrics'*, 1922). He asked 'what other purely English establishment than the Church, of sufficient dignity and footing, with such strength of old association, such scope for transmutability, such architectural spell, is left in this country to keep the shreds of morality together?' Although he called it 'forlorn' Hardy did cling to some hope of eventual

135

Thomas Hardy (right of the figure in the white surplice) attending an open-air church service.

improvement, 'of an alliance between religion, which must be retained unless the world is to perish, and complete rationality ... by means of the interfusing effect of poetry'.

**Return of the Native, The.** Written mostly at 'Riverside Villa', a quiet house by the Stour, near Sturminster Newton,★ in 1877–8 and altered considerably from its original conception. After Leslie Stephen★ had rejected it as 'dangerous for a family magazine', it was serialized in *Belgravia* from February 1878 to January 1879. The three-volume first-edition published by Smith, Elder and Co. on 4 November 1878 in an edition of 1,000 copies at 31s. 6d. was not an immediate success and 22 copies were remaindered. An early reviewer called it, 'very original, very gloomy, very great in some respects, though these respects are not the highest'.

The justly-famous Egdon★ Heath, remote, primeval and harshly beautiful, is inhabited by nineteenth-century characters. Clym Yeobright,★ an inflexible idealist, returns to his native Egdon and a disastrous romance with Eustacia Vye,★ a passionate dreamer. Their marriage provokes a fatal breach between Clym and his possessive mother, Mrs Yeobright,★ and scenes of bitter recrimination dominate this tragedy of rebellion.

The familiar rustics take their place on Egdon★ heath but Wessex★ has been invaded by modern consciousness bringing boredom, neurosis, and problematic sex. There is now the grim possibility that 'thought is a disease of the flesh'. The extravagant narrative style often conveys a dreamlike impression, 'as one might enter a brilliant chamber after a nightwalk in a wood'. The novel's power lies neither in its exploration of modern ideas nor in the creation of Egdon heath but in its human characters,★ especially the three women whose lives are deeply affected by the return of the native. *The Return of the Native* closes with an account of Clym's future as an 'itinerant preacher on morally unimpeachable themes' but the reader is haunted by the memory of Eustacia's face which, after her death by drowning, wore a pleasant expression, 'as if a sense of dignity had just compelled her to leave off speaking'.

Gertrude Bugler★ gave a memorable performance as Eustacia Vye in the Hardy Players'★ 1920 production of *The Return of the Native*, a scene from which was given before Hardy at Max Gate.★

The MS is in the library of University College, Dublin (National University of Ireland).

**Roads.** Hardy had a poetic feeling for roads. As a child he walked every day to Dorchester and back along country roads, felt the

The old road from Dorchester to Weymouth, by Hermann Lea.

The road to Eggardon hill today.

important presence of the adjacent London road, and the great antiquity of many Dorset thoroughfares. In 'The Roman Road' he recalls not pacing legionaries but his mother guiding his infant steps along the road. In later years, he cycled, and then motored along roads in an ever widening radius from Dorchester. Hardy's novels often open with wayfarers on the road and in *The Mayor of Casterbridge*★ the self-exiled Henchard★ works on the old Wessex highway to feel nearer to Elizabeth-Jane★ even though she is 50 miles down it from where he is working.

**Robin, Fanny** (*Far From the Madding Crowd*). A poor servant whose character was her destiny and who received more consideration after her death (in childbirth to the offspring of her seducer, Sergeant Troy) than during her short life. 'Perhaps Mrs Troy is right', observed Parson Thirdly beside Fanny's flower-decked coffin, 'in feeling that we cannot treat a dead fellow-creature too thoughtfully.'

**Roman Gravemounds, The.** In this touching poem Hardy assumes that someone carrying a basket and spade near a Roman gravemound is an archaeologist only to discover he is a pet-lover about to bury his dead cat, 'a little white furry thing, stiff of limb'. The poem was occasioned by the death of Kitsey, Hardy's 'study cat' who used 'to sleep on my writing table on any clean sheets of paper, and be much with me'.

**Romantic Adventures of A Milkmaid, The.** A perfunctory but still occasionally impressive story involving a Cinderella-like heroine and mixing realism and romance. It was hastily written in the winter of 1882–3 in Wimborne* and widely pirated in America before Hardy collected it in *A Changed Man** (1913).

**Rome.** Hardy visited Rome in the spring of 1887 and stayed in the Via Condotti, a street opposite the Piazza di Spagna, near the house where Keats* died. He declared himself more interested in pagan than in Christian Rome and formed vivid impressions of statues flared by sunsets, dust-covered trees in the Pincio contrasting with orange trees in sheltered gardens,* and an overpowering presence of decay in the crumbling walls and buildings. The highlight for him was to visit the graves of Shelley* and Keats, 'those matchless singers'.

**Ruined Maid, The.** The poem presents a dramatic dialogue between a country girl and her 'ruined' friend whom she meets in town. Questioned about her glamorous life, the friend answers in the refrains which are modified each time (' "Some polish is gained with one's ruin", said she') to provide both humour and a touching awareness of the sadness of her life.

**Ruskin, John** (1819–1900). An influential Victorian aesthete, art critic, and social reformer. Hardy's noting of 'the greatest thing a human soul ever does in this world is to *see* something, and tell what it *saw* in a plain way', from Ruskin's *Modern Painters* (1843–60) places him as an *observer* of things. His theory of the Gothic* art-principle shows the influence of *The Stones of Venice* (1851–3).

**Rustic Chorus.** Hardy's rustic chorus belongs to a tradition rooted in Shakespeare.* The Mellstock Quire, the turf-cutters of Egdon* Heath, the Casterbridge gossips, the regulars at Warren's malt-house, the cottagers in the woodlands of Hintock all enrich their novels with the perspective of humdrum daily life. They pass sobering comments on the high endeavours of the heroes and heroines and provide an inexhaustible source of humour.

Members of the Mellstock Quire in the Salisbury Playhouse production of *Under the Greenwood Tree*, 1978.

# S

**St Cleeve, Swithin** (*Two on a Tower*). A handsome but rather literal-minded young astronomer who proved a reluctant lover of his ardent patroness, Lady Viviette Constantine★ ('There was a certain scientific practicality even in his love-making'), and learnt too late the importance of human feelings.

**St Juliot** (West Endlestow). A granite church and a secluded rectory near Boscastle,★ Cornwall, where Hardy met Emma Lavinia Gifford in 1870. Her memoirs (*Some Recollections*★) describe this romantic spot, 'with beautiful sea-coast, and the wild Atlantic ocean rolling in with its magnificent waves and spray, its white gulls and black choughs and grey puffins, its cliffs and rocks and gorgeous sunsettings sparkling redness in a track widening from the horizon to the shore'. St Juliot was an emotional focal point for Hardy to which he returned in his imagination again and again.

Church at St Juliot.

The rectory at St Juliot where Hardy first met Emma Lavinia Gifford.

**Sacred to the Memory.** This short poem commemorates Hardy's sister Mary Hardy who died in 1915. He had the words 'Sacred to the memory of Mary, elder daughter of Thomas and Jemima Hardy' inscribed on her grave at Stinsford. The 'bare conventionality' of the inscription can never adequately recall Mary's life which is expressed in the 'landscape high and low / Wherein she made such worthy show'.

**Salisbury** (Melchester). A beautiful cathedral city built in the thirteenth century at the meeting point of four rivers sheltered by the downland of Wiltshire. Hardy regarded its graceful cathedral as the most marked instance in English architecture of an intention carried out to the full. The poem 'A Cathedral Facade at Midnight' describes the West front by moonlight.

**Sassoon, Siegfried** (1886–1967). Kentish-born poet whose satirical war★ poetry emerged from his experiences of the horror and futility of the Great War. His fictionalized memoirs reveal the conflicts created by the violent loss of his quiet, orderly, country-gentleman's life. In *Memoirs of an Infantry Officer* (1930) he describes

Siegfried Sassoon.

himself 'huddled up in a little dog-kennel of a dug-out reading *Tess of the D'Urbervilles'.*★ In 1919 he organized a tribute to Hardy from 43 poets in honour of his 79th birthday. His poem 'Max Gate'★ gives a charming picture of the 'old wizard of Wessex'.

**Satires of Circumstance, Lyrics and Reveries.** Hardy's fourth volume of verse, published by Macmillan in an edition of 2,000 copies at 4*s.* 6*d.* on 17 November 1914, contains 107 poems grouped under Lyrics and Reveries, Poems of 1912–13,★ Miscellaneous Pieces, Satires of Circumstance. It is his most widely read and quoted volume.

Lytton Strachey's review in *New Statesman* (19 December 1914) recognized Hardy's modern voice bringing 'the realism and sobriety of prose into the service of his poetry ... He is incorrect; but then how unreal and artificial a thing is correctness!'

The MSS, given by Hardy to Florence Hardy on her birthday, 12 January 1923, is now in the Dorset County Museum.

**'Schools of Painting' Notebook.** Hardy's earliest surviving notebook, dated 12 May 1863, written in London while he was working for Arthur Blomfield,★ carefully lists the artists of various schools adding brief comments ('Paolo Uccello – corrected perspective errors').

**Schopenhauer, Arthur** (1788–1860). German 'critical' philosopher who expressed his authentic pessimism★ with wit and elegance and whose doctrine of the deterministic tyranny of the will is expounded in *The World as Will and Idea* (1818). His influence on Hardy, best regarded as literary rather than philosophical, shows in *The Dynasts,*★ and the poem 'The Thing Unplanned'. In *Tess,*★ Angel Clare's★ father has a 'renunciative philosophy which had cousinship with that of Schopenhauer ...'

**Science of Fiction, The.** Hardy's essay argues that the science of fiction lies in selectivity, in capturing the essence of things rather than in the meticulous presentation of external details. (*New Review*, April 1891.)

**Scott, Sir Walter** (1771–1832). A legendary story-teller whose novels and poems achieved immediate popularity both at home and abroad. The young Hardy, although not directly influenced by Scott, identified with him in the epigraph to *Desperate Remedies,*★ quoting the dictum that 'the province of the romance-writer being artificial, there is more required from him than a mere compliance with the simplicity of reality'.

**Selected Poems.** A selection of 120 poems from *The Dynasts*★ and Hardy's first three volumes of verse, which Hardy hoped would reach a wider public, was published by Macmillan on 3 October 1916. One of Hardy's last literary activities was to prepare a new edition of *Selected Poems* in September 1927.

**Select Poems of William Barnes.** Hardy selected and edited this edition of Barnes'★ poetry which was published by Henry Frowde on 24 November 1908. In his introduction Hardy describes Barnes' use of dialect★ and refers to his 'closeness of phrase to vision' – words which convey the essence of Hardy's own poetry.

**Self-Unconscious, The.** The 'way' mentioned in the first line of this poem lies between Bossiney and Boscastle,★ a scene indelibly imprinted on Hardy's mind, the slaty sea visible across the fields, the lane alive with bright yellow-hammers carrying straws in their beaks. The image of straw-bearing yellow-hammers also occurs in the poem 'The Yellow-Hammers'★ and in *The Mayor of Casterbridge*★ when Michael Henchard★ walks on 'in silent thought unheeding the yellow-hammers which flitted about the hedges with straws in their bills!'

Hardy reproaches himself for not really noticing these 'earth's artistries' in his absorption with plans of the moment (it is 1870, the year of his meeting with Emma★) and even more for lacking real self-knowledge at the time ('himself he did not see at all'). Hardy told Vere H. Collins★ that, 'If he had realized, when young, what he was, he would have acted differently. That is the tragedy of youth: when we know, it is too late to alter things.'

**Shakespeare, William** (1564–1616). Hardy's strange prediction in *The Life*★ (p. 341) that Shakespeare would survive as a poet rather than as a dramatist may have been the result of seeing the ponderous staging of Shakespeare then in vogue. His own rustic chorus displays a Shakespearian quality of earthy poetics.

**She Did Not Turn.** This poem illustrates Hardy's ability to create a powerful sense of physical presence by negatives: the opening lines; 'She did not turn / But passed foot-faint with averted head / In her gown of green, by the bobbing fern' are tense with movement and contrast: The woman seems more vividly present than if she *had* turned round.

**Shelley, Percy Bysshe** (1792–1822). Romantic poet whose pursuit of literary, sexual, and political freedom was violently cut short by his drowning in the Gulf of Spezia, Italy. Hardy admired Shelley more than any other poet, was greatly influenced by him, and made many allusions★ to his poetry. The scene in *A Pair of Blue Eyes*★ where Stephen Smith★ projects his ideal fantasy on to Elfride Swancourt★ as she sings Shelley's 'When the Lamp is Shattered' in a glowing candlelit aureole was based on Hardy's memory of Emma★ at St Juliot★ rectory. It perfectly illustrates Shelley's belief that 'nothing exists but as it is perceived'.

**Sherborne** (Sherton Abbas). Sherborne, one-time Saxon capital and later a cathedral city, is rich in historic buildings including an imposing abbey in golden stone, two castles, an almshouse, old inns, sixteenth- and seventeenth-century houses, several famous schools, and museum. In *The Woodlanders*★ Hardy decribes Sherton Abbas on a bright morning as having 'the linear distinctness of architectural drawings, as if the original dream and vision of the conceiving master-mason were for a brief hour flashed down through the centuries to an appreciative age'.

**Short-Stories.** Hardy wrote nearly 50 short-stories, a substantial body of work. Some were hurriedly turned out on demand for magazines and are slight productions though rarely without interest. At their best the short-stories convey a congenial atmosphere of fire-side tales, folklore, and legend. They show Hardy in a relaxed vein, unburdened by attempts to philosophize. Stories of the quality of 'Fellow Townsmen',★ 'A Tragedy of Two Ambitions',★ 'On The Western Circuit',★ 'The Fiddler of the Reels',★ 'An Imaginative Woman'★ and 'For Conscience' Sake'★ put in question Hardy's supposed indifference to the short-stories and critical neglect of them. While his narrative mode suited the space afforded by a novel he is such a born story-teller that he often succeeds within the confined space of a short-story. Had Hardy written no novels, his short-stories would be much more highly regarded.

**Slow Nature, The.** This ballad★ poem 'brings the Froom valley before our eyes' (Hermann Lea)★ as well as involving us in a psychological drama. A farm-woman, loathe to believe a report that her husband has been killed by a bull, realizes the arrival of his body is imminent and shocks the simple messenger by thinking first 'of her unkempt room'.

Only later do her deeper emotions find expression and she 'pined in a slow decay'. Hardy observed in himself a tendency towards the delayed expression of emotion.

Thomas Hardy in middle age.

**Smith, Stephen** (*A Pair of Blue Eyes*). A young architect who quickly acquired 'any kind of knowledge he saw around him' but whose humble origins proved an obstacle to his marrying Elfride Swancourt.* He elopes with her to London but she panics on Paddington station declaring, 'I don't like it here – nor myself – nor you!' He achieved success and status in India but in the meantime lost the love of Elfride to his friend and mentor Henry Knight.* He returns to India. He finds himself irresistibly drawn back to Elfride and travels down to Cornwall on a train which is, unknown to him, also bearing Elfride – in her coffin! Hardy took pains, in *The Life*,* to deny the suggestion that Stephen Smith was a self-portrait.

**Some Recollections.** A small volume of reminiscences by Emma Hardy,* written a few years before her death, which Hardy found on going through her papers. He quoted part of it in *The Life*ic* but it was not published in full until 1961. *Some Recollections* is a charming and spontaneous evocation of Victorian life in the West Country showing Emma's love of people and places. She recalls her happy Plymouth* childhood, her zestful days in Cornwall, 'scampering up and down the hills on my beloved mare alone', and the romantic meeting with her husband ('I thought he was much older than he was'). Hardy's discovery of *Some Recollections* was the catalyst, partly, for the flood of love poems (Poems 1912–23*) which followed soon after. The MSS is in the Dorset County Museum.

**Some Romano-British Relics.** Hardy read this paper to the Dorchester meeting of the Dorset Natural History and Antiquarian Field Club on 13 May 1884. It describes the urns and skeletons found while digging the foundations for his house at Max Gate.*

**Somerset, George** (*A Laodicean*). A young architect with an interest in poetry and religion* who is reminiscent of the young Hardy in the way 'poetry, theology, and the reorganization of society had seemed matters of more importance to him than a profession'. His fidelity to the heroine, Paula Power,* through lengthy vicissitudes is eventually rewarded.

**Son's Veto, The.** In this moving story a vicar's widow (formerly his parlour-maid) is prevented from marrying her first love, a market-gardener's assistant, at the insistence of her educated and socially ambitious son. From her semi-detached villa she watches the country waggons passing with loads of vegetables for Covent Garden. 'How the fresh green-stuff brightened to life as it came opposite the lamp.' Then, as though by a charm, she realizes that one of the waggoners is her former lover but the son's veto prevails. The story was first printed in *Illustrated London News*, 1 December 1891, and later collected in *Life's Little Ironies** (1894).

**South, John** (*The Woodlanders*). An old man who developed an obsessive fear that a tall elm tree opposite his bedroom would crash down on him. The tree was cut down by stealth one night on the advice of Dr Fitzpiers.* When John South saw the blank space instead of his familiar anxiety his terror at the change was even greater and he died of shock. 'Damned if my remedy hasn't killed him!' murmured Fitzpiers.

**South, Marty** (*The Woodlanders*). A woodland girl whose face had 'the usual fullness of expression which is developed by a life of solitude'. Her observation of things, kindness, humility, and devotion make her a chorus-like figure. She comes into her own when, standing by Giles Winterborne's* grave, she utters a beautiful lament. '... But no, no, my love, I never can forget 'ee; for you was a good man, and did good things!'

**Sparks, Tryphena** (1851–90). Hardy's cousin, Tryphena, was born to James and Maria Sparks at Puddletown* on 20 March 1851. When Hardy returned to Higher Bockhampton* 16 years later she

Tryphena Sparks.

was a lively dark-haired beauty and he formed some kind of attachment to her. In 1870 she went to Stockwell Training College, later became headmistress of Plymouth* Public Free School, married Charles Gale of Topsham, Exeter, and had four children. She died on 17 March 1890 three days before her thirty-ninth birthday. Hardy described her in 'Thoughts of Phena' as 'my lost prize'. In *Providence and Mr Hardy* (1966) Lois Deacon, mainly on the oral testimony of Tryphena's daughter, Mrs Eleanor Bromwell (1878–1965), claims that Tryphena was Hardy's niece, was engaged to him, and had his child; these conjectures have been challenged by Robert Gittings in *Young Thomas Hardy* (1975).

**Spectre of the Real, The.** Hardy wrote this story in collaboration with Florence Henniker* in 1893. The work was mostly Hardy's and Mrs Henniker helped with the plot and with textual revision. Hardy wrote to his collaborator expecting 'all the wickedness (if it has any) will be attributed to you'. The story, published in *To-Day* in 1894, was badly received and no MS has survived.

**Spencer, Herbert** (1820–1903). Founder of evolutionary philosophy★ and champion of the rights of the individual providing he respects the rights of other individuals. Spencer's *First Principles* (1862) provided the germ for Hardy's notions about the Immanent Will in *The Dynasts*.★

**Springrove, Edward** (*Desperate Remedies*). Architect and poet of humble origin with 'a keen sense of having been passed in the race by men whose brains are nothing to his own, all through his seeing too far into things'. After unmasking the villain he rescued and married Cytherea Graye.★ Although Hardy says in *The Life*,★ that he modelled Springrove on a fellow-assistant at Crickmay's drawing-office in Weymouth★ he also resembles Hardy. The delightful boating-scene, in which Springrove shares his thoughts with his charming passenger, Cytherea Graye, telling her that, 'worldly advantage from an art doesn't depend upon mastering it', was almost certainly based on Hardy's own experiences at Weymouth.

**Stephen, Sir Leslie** (1832–1904). A Victorian man of letters, athlete, mountaineer who was the father of Virginia Woolf★ by a second marriage. He was first editor of *The Dictionary of National Biography* (begun 1882) and contributed entries for eighteenth- and

Leslie Stephen with his daughter, Virginia.

nineteenth-century figures. While editor of *Cornhill Magazine* he encouraged Hardy to persevere as a novelist, made judicious criticisms, and published *Far From the Madding Crowd* ★ and *The Hand of Ethelberta*. ★ On 23 March 1875 he called upon Hardy to witness his formal renunciation of the holy orders he had taken as a young man in Cambridge. cf. 'The Schreckhorn'.

**Stevenson, Robert Louis** (1850–94). Much-travelled writer best known for *Treasure Island* (1883) and *The Strange Case of Dr Jekyll and Mr Hyde* (1886). Hardy contributed a brief memoir to *I Can Remember Robert Louis Stevenson* (1922) and revealed that Stevenson once asked his permission to dramatize *The Mayor of Casterbridge*. ★

**Stinsford** (Mellstock). A scattered amalgam of three hamlets, four large houses, several farms and a church. Although only one and a half miles east of Dorchester, ★ Stinsford still preserves an air of remoteness. Hardy loved the small church of St Michael and his heart is buried in the churchyard. 'Stinsford was a favourite haunt until the last few months of his life . . . and the churchyard was to him the most hallowed spot on earth.' cf. 'A Church Romance' and 'Afternoon Service at Mellstock'.

The churchyard at Stinsford.

**Stonehenge.** This awe-inspiring Bronze Age monument, completed *c.* 1400 BC, is powerfully integrated into the story of *Tess of the D'Urbervilles*★ to provide the setting of one of Hardy's most moving scenes: the parting of Tess from Angel, and from Hardy's imagination. An interview with Hardy, 'Shall Stonehenge Go?', reported in the *Daily Chronicle*, 24 August 1899, is contained in *Thomas Hardy's Personal Writings* (edited Orel, 1966).

**Study of Thomas Hardy.** D. H. Lawrence★ began this brilliant, idiosyncratic essay in September 1914 'enraged by the war' and insisting it would be 'about anything but Thomas Hardy'. The essay, as well as passionately diagnosing contemporary sickness and searching for cures, contains some marvellous insights into the fundamental natures of Hardy's characters.★ Lawrence argues that as soon as a Hardy character 'weary of the stage ... looks into the wilderness raging round ... he is lost, his little drama falls to pieces, it becomes mere repetition, but the stupendous theatre outside goes on enacting its own incomprehensible drama, untouched'. The essay was finished in 1914, and published posthumously in 1936 (Phoenix).

**Sturminster Newton** (Stourcastle). A spacious market-town on the River Stour in north-east Dorset with a castle-mound, church, market-place, and picturesque mill. Hardy lived here from 1876–8 and spent the 'happiest days' of his marriage★ while writing *The Return of the Native*.★ cf. 'Overlooking the River Stour', 'A Two Years Idyll', 'A Musical Box'.

**Style.** In Hardy's view, 'The whole secret of style lies in not having too much style – being in fact a little careless ...' (*The Life*★).

**Sunshade, The.** The primitive habit of confusing persons and things informs this stark poem. The skeleton of a lady's sunshade, exposed to the noonday sun, eclipses the more significant recollection of the lady who carried it.

**Supernatural.** Hardy was temperamentally drawn to premonitions, omens, telepathy, prophecies, psychic phenomena but regarded them as natural. Rather than believe in the supernatural he believed in science. He would (according to William Archer) have given ten years of his life to see a ghost but could find no evidence for them. Thus Hardy quizzes and scrutinizes everything that he can observe.

**Swanage** (Knollsea). A sea-side town in south-east Dorset,★ once a small fishing village, turned into a fashionable watering-place after a visit by Princess Victoria in 1835. The coming of the railway★ in the 1880s produced a boarding-house boom and early this century Hermann Lea★ complained of 'the blatant style of architecture which utterly spoils the ancient picturesqueness of the place'. Hardy stayed there at West End cottage with Emma in the winter of 1875–6 while completing *The Hand of Ethelberta*.★ cf. 'Once at Swanage', 'To a Sea-Cliff'.

**Swancourt, Elfride** (*A Pair of Blue Eyes*). A clergyman's daughter (she often wrote her father's sermons) with eyes 'as blue as Autumn distance'. She had the misfortune to fall in love with two men who were friends and, in different ways, inadequate lovers. Her terrible illusion of freedom, symbolized in her dropping the reins of her horse to allow the beast to decide which direction she should take, is ruthlessly exposed by Fate. She is trapped in a country region of the utmost spaciousness and grandeur. It is ironic that Emma Hardy,★ in some ways the model for Elfride, should have found a man to take her away from the same setting only to feel later that she had been uprooted.

**Swinburne, Algernon Charles** (1837–1909). A lyrical poet who startled Victorian London with melodious verses on the darker, crueller side of love (*Ballads and Poems*, 1866). The young Hardy responded enthusiastically to this fresh poetic voice and read him while walking the streets of London. 'It was as though a garland of roses / Had fallen about the hood of some smug nun'. Swinburne, who also wrote literary criticism, described *Jude*★ as 'equally beautiful and terrible in its pathos'. In 1910 Hardy visited Swinburne's grave at Bonchurch, on the Isle of Wight, and wrote the elegy 'A Singer Asleep' which evokes Swinburne's obsession with the sea.

**Symbolism.** A literary movement originating in late nineteenth-century France which included such poets as Verlaine, Rimbaud, and Mallarmé. By use of symbols – things that stand for something else – the symbolist works by allusion and suggestion, rather than direct meaning. At best symbolism conveys a sense of mystery and expansiveness; at its worst it is obscure and esoteric.

Hardy, a very literal-minded artist, strongly rooted in place and time, who might seem unaffected by such modernist movements, accommodates symbolism quite naturally into his poetry.

# T

**Tennyson, Alfred Lord** (1809–92). Victorian poet laureate, master of mood, elegaic, technically flawless, who in his lifetime received more veneration than any other living English poet. Hardy met him in London in 1880 and often regretted that, though warmly invited he never visited Tennyson at Farringford, his Isle of Wight home. Hardy and Emma★ read Tennyson together in the grounds of St Juliot★ rectory and Hardy quotes in his journal Tennyson's line 'The tender grace of a day that is dead' to describe the end of a happy outing to Beeny Cliff.★

Alfred Lord Tennyson.

**Tess of the D'Urbervilles.** *Tess of the D'Urbervilles: A Pure Woman.* Faithfully presented by Thomas Hardy, was written at Max Gate★ in 1888–9 and is regarded by many critics and readers as Hardy's masterpiece. It had a turbulent publication history. The first version, called *Too Late, Beloved!*, had reached the half-way stage when Hardy's refusal to make certain alterations led to a cancellation of the contract with Tillotson. Two further rejections, by Murray's

153

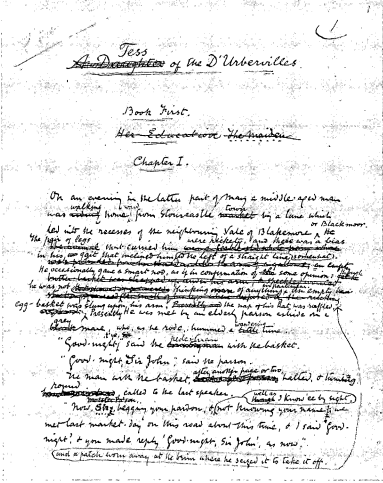

The first page of *Tess* in MS, now in the British Library.

and Macmillan's Magazines, saw Hardy resign himself, 'with cynical amusement', to bowdlerizing the story and *Tess of the D'Urbervilles* minus the seduction scene was serialized in the *Graphic* between July and December 1891. Hardy was able 'to piece the trunk and limbs of the novel together' for the first edition published in three-volumes by Osgood, McIlvaine and Co. on 29 November 1891 in an edition of 1,000 copies at 31s. 6d. It was an immediate success, making Hardy rich for life.

The folk-ballad★ plot – Tess's abandonment and betrayal by her husband, Angel Clare,★ and subjection by her former seducer, Alec D'Urberville,★ for whose murder she is hunted down and hanged – is transcended by the rich narrative texture and Tess's wonderful vitality in the midst of all forms of death. Wandering amid 'the oozing fatness and warm ferments of the Froom Vale at a season when the rush of juices could almost be heard', Tess partakes of the ripeness and fertility of her surroundings. The novel explores the upheavals of rural and social change, the commonplace realities of work and daily life, but it is pre-eminently the story of 'a woman living her precious life'. In Tess, Hardy's 'feeling, his instinct, his sensuous understanding' found a perfect counterpart, and she is in the words of Irving Howe 'that rare creature in literature, goodness made interesting'.

There have been many dramatizations of *Tess*. Lorimer Stoddard's version with Mrs Fiske as Tess was produced at the Fifth Avenue Theatre, New York, 2 March 1897. An opera version by Baron Frederic d'Erlanger, had its premiere at San Carlos, Naples, in 1906 and was interrupted by an eruption of Mount Vesuvius. A ludicrous film-version by MGM in 1924, with Blanche Sweet as Tess, had her meeting Alec in a night-club. Hardy's version was produced in Dorchester★ by the Hardy Players★ in 1924 with Gertrude Bugler★ as Tess. Other actresses who have played Tess include Gwen Frangcon-Davies (Barnes and Garrick Theatres, London, 1926), Wendy Hiller (Bristol Old Vic, 1946), Barbara Jefford (BBC TV 1952), Geraldine McEwan (ITV 1960.) Roman Polanski's film of *Tess*, released in 1979, with Nastassia Kinski as Tess has reached a world-wide audience. The MS was presented by Hardy to the British Museum in 1911.

**Texts.** Hardy's novels★ underwent considerable revisions before the definitive Wessex★ Edition (24 vols., London, 1912–31). Hardy had the habit of using commas sparingly and wrote stretches of lightly punctuated prose to convey the rhythms of the narrative or speaking voice. Simon Gatrell's essay 'Hardy, House-Style, and the Aesthetics of Punctuation' (*The Novels of Thomas Hardy* edited Anne Smith, London 1979) suggests that compositors added commas to Hardy's text to such an extent that there is a need for editions which will restore Hardy's original punctuation.

**Theatre.** Hardy maintained an active interest in the theatre and when in London was a regular theatregoer. His *Why I Don't Write*

Hardy discusses the role of Tess with Gwen Ffrangcon-Davies. Florence Hardy is in the background.

*Plays* (Pall Mall Gazette, 1892) criticized contemporary preoccupation' with elaborate staging and his conception of *The Queen of Cornwall*★ anticipated the modern theatre-in-the-round. He was involved in several attempts to present his novels, especially *Tess*,★ on the stage. (cf. *'Tess' in the Theatre* edited Marguerite Roberts, Toronto, 1950.)

**Thomas, Edward** (1878–1917). English nature poet, encouraged to write by Robert Frost, who was killed in action at Arras in 1917 before he acquired fame. His poems explore solitude and the intimate detail of the English countryside. Edward Thomas was quick to recognize Hardy's greatness as a poet and saw that, despite his fatalism,★ 'he was further from surrender than might appear in some poems'. He published two essays on Hardy *In Pursuit of Spring* (1914) and *A Literary Pilgrim* (1917).

**Three Strangers, The.** In this story a christening-party in a remote farmhouse is invaded by three strangers – a hangman on his way to Casterbridge gaol, his unrecognized victim who has just escaped and the condemned man's brother. Hardy, who had twice witnessed public hangings, neatly contrives the fugitive's escape. This story from *Wessex Tales*★ (1888) exploits Hardy's knowledge of tradition and legend.

**Three Wayfarers, The.** Hardy's one-act dramatization from the story *The Three Strangers*, undertaken at J. M. Barrie's★ suggestion, first performed in 1893 at Terry's Theatre, London, and by the Hardy Players★ in 1911. Hardy later described the work as 'a mere trifle I would be horrified to write now'. No MS survives.

**Time.** Hardy showed an acute awareness of time. As a child he expressed a wish not to grow up and later in life resented the lack of synchronization between the pace of his inner life and that of the clock-bound world. 'I am content with tentativeness from day to day,' he wrote when he was 43.

An illustration by Hardy for
*Wessex Poems.*

In one of Hardy's most gripping scenes, Elizabeth-Jane★ in *The Mayor of Casterbridge*★ keeps vigil by her dying mother. 'Between the hours at which the last toss-pot went by and the first sparrow shook himself, the silence in Casterbridge – barring the rare sound of the watchman – was broken in Elizabeth's ear only by the time-piece in the bedroom ticking frantically against the clock on the stairs, ticking harder and harder till it seemed to clang like a gong; and all this while the subtle-souled girl was asking herself why she was born, why sitting in a room, and blinking at the candle; why things around her had taken the shape they wore in preference to every other possible shape.' Hardy's time-conscious novels★ require that we adjust ourselves to their movement.

Hardy, who lived for 88 years, took time to discover himself as a writer. His hurried to-ing and fro-ing between Dorset★ and

London* induced the breakdown which interrupted the writing of *A Laodicean*. In the latter novel Paula Power* says that 'time, being so much more valuable now, must of course be cut up into smaller pieces'.

**Time's Laughingstocks and Other Verses.** Hardy's third volume of verse, containing 94 poems, was published by Macmillan in an edition of 2,000 copies on 3 December 1909. The poems cover a period of 40 years and often concern people close to Hardy. Such tender reminiscences as 'Night in the Old Home'* and 'A Church Romance' confute the early reviewers' description of the volume as predominantly pessimistic. 'More Love Lyrics' concern, as well as Emma,* some other important women in his life – Tryphena Sparks,* Florence Henniker,* and Florence Dugdale.* There is a beautiful portrait of his paternal grandmother Mary Head* in 'One We Knew', 'Past things retold were to her as things existent / Things present but as a tale'. The MS is now in the Fitzwilliam Museum, Cambridge.

**Timing Her.** This ecstatic poem, written to an old folk-tune, sustains the excitement and anticipation of a visit from a comely girl called Lalage for the length of nine verses. 'Lalage's coming / She's nearer now, O / End anyhow, O, / Today's husbandry!'. The intensity of the poet's expectation could never be surpassed, one fears, by her actual presence.

**Tinsley, William** (1831–1902). Co-founder of Hardy's early publishers, Tinsley Brothers. Tinsley, a friendly and shrewd business man, offered Hardy £30 for the copyright of *Under the Greenwood Tree** which Hardy considered a 'trifle' but accepted. Later, when Tinsley negotiated for Hardy's next novel (*A Pair of Blue Eyes**), the wary young author read *Copinger on Copyright* overnight and the following day insisted that the contract cover the magazine-issue solely, after which all rights were to return to the author. 'Well, I'm damned!' Tinsley replied with a grim laugh.

**Tradition of Eighteen-Hundred and Four.** The narrator recounts a story told him by old Solomon Selby one rainy evening. England is threatened with invasion by Napoleon's army of 160,000 men and 15,000 horses in a couple of thousand flat-bottomed boats. On clear days, shepherds on the downs see the drilling going on across the channel, 'the accoutrements of the rank and file glittering in the sun like silver'. The only question now is, where will Bonaparte land?

One still night at Lullwind Cove, when the rise and fall of the tide could be heard every few minutes, 'like a sort of great snore of the sleeping world', Selby, then a young shepherd boy, and his uncle Job, see below them on the shore two foreigners scanning a map by lantern-light. A sudden upward glare reveals the unmistakable face of old Boney himself! 'His bullet head, his short neck, his round yaller cheeks and chin, his gloomy face, and his great glowing eyes.' Without his new-flint firelock uncle Job is powerless and the arch-enemy slips away.

Hardy's historical vision so creates the illusion of present events that we are surprised at the end to learn that old Solomon Selby has been beneath his grave-stone for the last ten years.

It was first printed in *Harper's* in 1882, included in *Life's Little Ironies*★ (1894), and transferred to *Wessex Tales*★ in 1912. Thirty-seven years after the story's first appearance Hardy learnt that his improbable tale of Napoleon's nocturnal visit was in fact a well-established tradition.

**Tragedy of Two Ambitions, A.** This story of two ambitious brothers thwarted by their drunken father concerns matters of religion and class which were very personal to Hardy. Florence Hardy★ regarded it as his best story. It was published in *The Universal Review* December 1888 and later collected in *Life's Little Ironies*★ (1894). In Dennis Potter's BBC television version in 1973 John Hurt played Joshua Halborough.

**Trampwoman's Tragedy, A.** An eerie ballad,★ with realistic settings framed in well-wrought stanzas, which tells how a trampwoman goaded her jealous lover into killing a rival by falsely attributing to him their expected child. The lover is hanged, the baby still-born, and the trampwoman roams the western moor alone, haunted by guilt and remorse. Hardy regarded it as 'upon the whole his most successful poem'.

**Transformations.** This short poem meditates on those buried in Stinsford★ churchyard 'surviving' in the yew trees, grass, or roses that grow from their graves; 'Portion of this yew / Is a man my grandsire knew'. Gerald Finzi's★ musical setting is in *A Young Man's Exhortations* (OUP, 1933).

**Translations.** Eugenio Montale, one of Hardy's translators, discovered that 'the intricate net that Hardy cast to encompass his poetry demands a saturation of monosyllables such as can be found only in the English language'. Hardy's novels have been more satisfactorily translated into other languages and *Tess*★ has been most widely translated.

**Trees.** Trees are the most familiar constituents of the Wessex★ landscape. Hardy's first poem 'Domicilium' described his birth-place canopied by high beeches which swept against the roof. Rarely are the trees of Wessex mere detached observers but, from the mysticism of 'stirless depths of the yews' in 'A Spellbound Palace' to the primitive violence of the tree in 'The Ivy-Wife' which 'Being bark-bound, flagged, snapped, fell outright' and kills the onlooker, the trees are involved with the events around them.

One recurring image – the rhythmic bending of boughs – is associated with Emma★ and his crucial parting from her beneath the trees at St Juliot.★

Ancient Yews, Bingham's Melcombe, Dorset, believed to date from c. 1530, photograph by Roger Mayne.

**Trollope, Anthony** (1815–82). A prolific and consistent novel-ist. Although he was an important official in the Post Office, Trollope found time to methodically write 250 words an hour for four hours a day. His novels enshrine the virtues of middle class English life. Hardy admired Trollope, especially the construction of *The Eustace Diamonds* (1873) and lent his copy of *Barchester Towers* (1857) to his sister Mary★ with the comment that it was considered his best work.

An article 'Trollope's Wheelbarrow in *Tess*:* The Decorum of Love' by Dale Kramer (Hardy Society Review, 1976) suggests that Hardy's revision in the serial version of *Tess* whereby Angel Clare wheels instead of carries Tess and her friends across a muddy lane has a precedent in Trollope's earlier novel Doctor Thorne (1858). There, too, a wheelbarrow is considered as an alternative to a physically closer means of transporting a female over mud.

**Troy, Francis** (*Far From the Madding Crowd*). An attractive adventurer and seducer who lived only for the moment. At the supreme crisis of his life, confronted with the consequences of his nature, 'he simply threw up his cards and foreswore his game for that time and always', leaving the author to kill him off in the service of the plot.

Sergeant Troy (Terence Stamp) in the film *Far From the Madding Crowd*.

**Trumpet–Major, The.** It was written at 1 Arundel Terrace, Upper Tooting, in 1879–80 after Hardy had thoroughly researched the period (see 'The Trumpet-Major' Notebook*). It was printed serially in *Good Words* from January to December 1880 and the three-volume first edition of 1,000 copies at 31s. 6d. was published by Smith, Elder and Co. on 26 October 1880. Reviews were favourable but it did not sell well at first and 33 copies were remaindered. It remains Hardy's most underrated novel.

*The Trumpet-Major* chronicles the lives of ordinary people caught up in extraordinary events (the Napoleonic wars and a threatened invasion) and tells the love-story of Anne Garland* and her three suitors through a series of highly coloured tableaux. Beneath the

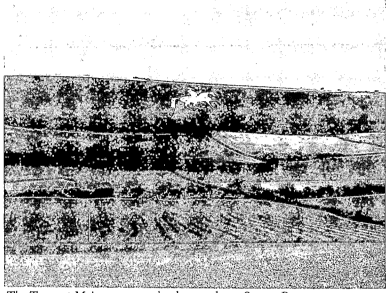

*The Trumpet-Major* country, the downs above Sutton Poyntz.

Roger Fenton's photograph of *The Victory*.

brilliant surface lies a sense of time* passing. Sudden switches of perspective reveal that a person described has long since vanished, part of 'that common human story which always has the same ending, that of death' (Barbara Hardy). On the last page the trumpet-major John Loveday,* having lost Anne to his brother Bob,* 'goes off to blow his trumpet till silenced for ever upon one of the bloody battlefields of Spain'. Although haunted by such melancholy moments the novel is primarily a lyrical comedy and it occupies a unique place in the Hardy canon.

Hardy sent a presentation copy to Queen Victoria on 6 December 1880. The MS was presented to King George V in 1911 and is now in the Royal Library, Windsor Castle.

**'Trumpet-Major' Notebook.** A small octavo notebook containing extensive data on the Napoleonic era gathered at the British Museum and elsewhere from 1878 onwards. Hardy's precise notes range from newspaper accounts of the time to meticulous details of military dress. It also provided material for *The Dynasts*.*

**Tryst at an Ancient Earthwork, A.** This story, first published in the *Detroit Post*, 1885, tells of a surreptitious archaeological dig at Mai-Dun on a stormy night. It contains one of Hardy's finest passages of sustained description in which the ancient earthwork is likened to an antediluvian creature, 'lying life-less, and covered with a thin green cloth, which hides its substance, while revealing its contour...'

**Turner, Joseph Mallord William** (1775–1851). English painter whose early period contained both classical and romantic elements and whose mature, experimental style partly anticipated the twentieth century. Hardy mentions Turner's work twice in the novels and four times in his *Notebooks** ('What he paints chiefly is light as modified by objects'). There is a 'Turneresque' quality in many of Hardy's verbal landscapes. In *Tess,** for example, written after a visit to Italy, Hardy described the Frome water-meadows as drenched in 'spectral, half-compounded, aqueous light' and the Arctic-like snowscapes of Flintcombe-Ash as an 'achromatic chaos of things'.

**Two on a Tower.** This tragi-comic romance was written at 'Llanherne', Wimborne,* for serialization in *The Atlantic Monthly* (Boston) and simultaneously in England. 'The actual writing was lamentably hurried – having been produced month by month' (letter to Gosse*). It was published in three volumes by Sampson

Low in October 1882 in an edition of 1,000 copies at 31s. 6d.

Some critics were offended by the heroine's cynical marriage to a bishop to legitimize her unborn child. *The Saturday Review* conceded that 'strange behaviour is less startling on the top of an astronomical tower than in an ordinary drawing-room'.

The novel concentrates on two central characters, Lady Viviette Constantine,★ a lonely, warm-hearted woman, who falls in love with a dedicated young astronomer, Swithin St Cleeve.★ He is slow to respond because 'his heaven at present was truly in the skies'. Hardy's wish 'to set the emotional history of two infinitesimal lives against the stupendous background of the stellar universe' (1895 Preface) is imaginatively realized but sometimes it seems obviously 'got up' by a fast-working professional (this was Hardy's seventh novel in ten years).

For all its unevenness, the poetic texture of *Two on a Tower* is never broken and carries us to a moving ending. Swithin returns from a long absence spent studying the vast interstellar spaces. Such distances are themselves eclipsed by the re-united lovers' awareness of the age-gap now opened up between them. '. . . instead of rushing forward to her he had stood still; and there appeared upon his face a look which there was no mistaking.'

The MS is now in the Houghton Library, Harvard.

# U

**Under the Greenwood Tree.** *Under the Greenwood Tree*, subtitled *A Rural Painting of the Dutch School*, incorporated material from an earlier discarded novel (*The Poor Man and the Lady*). It was written rapidly, finished in the summer of 1871, and offered to Macmillan★ who rejected it as 'very slight and rather unexciting'. Tinsley★ offered £30 for the copyright and Hardy promptly accepted.

It was published anonymously in two volumes on 15 June 1872 in an edition of 500 copies at 21s. Despite good reviews and a modest advertising campaign it did not sell well. Later, the now popular author sought to buy back the copyright; the price suggested was £300.

*Under the Greenwood Tree*, set in the countryside directly around Hardy's childhood home in Higher Bockhampton,★ is an idyllic

Salisbury Playhouse production of *Under the Greenwood Tree*, 1978.

pastoral★ comedy. The romance of Dick Dewy★ and Fancy Day★ provides gossip for the Mellstock Quire, a community still secure in a recurring pattern of work and play. A few shadows fall across this sunlit story – the passing of youth, rural decline, change – but the warm humanity of the Mellstock Quire prevails. The novel also celebrates everyday and seasonal life, especially spring 'when country people go to bed among nearly naked trees ... and awake next morning among green ones; when the landscape appears embarrassed with the weight and brilliancy of its leaves ...' It is Hardy's happiest novel.

The MS bears an inscription from Hardy to his second wife who bequeathed it to the Dorset County Museum.★

**Under the Waterfall.** This poem is based on an incident when Emma★ dropped a tiny picnic-tumbler into a brook 'and there it is to be found to this day no doubt between two small boulders' (*Some Recollections*★). The emotions of that 'fugitive day' become indistinguishable from the immediacy, colours, sounds, and tangibility of the physical details. Their love was 'consecrated' by the lost cup 'which no lip has touched ... since his and mine'.

Sketch by Thomas Hardy of Emma searching for the picnic-tumbler.

Entrance to the Vallency valley where the tumbler was lost.

# V

**Venice.** Hardy found more pleasure in Venice during his Italian tour of 1887 than in any other city previously visited. The short-story *Alicia's Diary*,★ written soon afterwards, pictures the sea-girt buildings 'floating raft-like on the smooth, blue deep'. For all the visionary splendour there Hardy said he brought to it, in his person, the solidity of Dorchester★ and Wessex★ life. The bell of the Campanile of St Marco reminded him of the peculiar timbre given out by the bells of Puddletown.★

**Venn, Diggory** (*The Return of the Native*). An 'isolated and weird' reddleman whose grotesque appearance 'in tight raiment and red from top to toe', which he acquired supplying dye to sheep-farmers, concealed a gallant selflessness. He remained loyal to Thomasin Yeobright★ after she had rejected him and married her in the end. (*The Return of the Native.*)

**Voice, The.** One of the 'Poems 1912–13'★ expressing Hardy's loss of the woman who still calls to him beyond the grave. He remembers her in every detail, 'even to the original air-blue gown!' The break-down of rhythm in the last stanza seems a direct communication from the poet that dispenses with the need for artifice.

**Vye, Eustacia** (*The Return of the Native*). A passionate and restless

Illustration of Eustacia Vye by Peter Whiteman.

girl, daughter of a Corfiote bandmaster at Budmouth, transplanted to lonely Egdon★ heath. There she fiercely nourishes her grandiose aspirations (symbolized by the telescope she often carried with her), idealizes Damon Wildeve★ 'for want of a better object' until Clym Yeobright's★ return from Paris better feeds her romantic visions. She marries Clym, quickly tires of his pedantry and renews her meetings with Wildeve. Tragic misunderstandings hasten the complete breakdown of any viable life for her on Egdon and she is drowned trying to escape from it. She is Hardy's most theatrical heroine who nevertheless seems touchingly human in her moments of high anger or despair.

# W

**Waiting Supper, The.** The supper of the story-title has been prepared for Christine Everard and Nicholas Long, her first love, on the eve of their wedding (made possible by the death of Christine's first husband). After a clock has crashed ominously to the floor a messenger brings word of the imminent arrival of Christine's first husband who is not dead after all. Nicholas departs and Christine drearily awaits the re-union. Her husband never arrives. It is 17 years before the lovers learn that the absent husband who has kept them apart lies drowned in the weir piles outside the house. Christine suggests it is hardly worthwhile to marry after so many years. Nicholas 'ventured to urge her to reconsider the case, though he spoke not with the fervour of his earlier years'. *The Waiting Supper* after magazine publication in 1887–8 was collected in *A Changed Man* (1913).★

**War.** Graphic pages in *The Life,*★ written after the declaration of the Great War, 'the streets hot and sad, and bustling with soldiers and recruits', show Hardy patriotically trying to raise morale while regarding war itself with abhorrence and disgust. His war poetry – covering the Napoleonic Wars, the Boer War, the Great War – declines in quality the more recent the war treated: he is too close and anguished to write well about the latter war. Where his imagination is freed by distance the results are impressive. *The Dynasts*★ recreates the actual sensations and sights of battle. 'The worm asks what can be overhead / And wriggles deep from a scene so grim /

Devastated landscape of the Great War.

and guesses him safe; for he does not know / What a foul red flood will be soaking him!'. The 'War Poems' section of *Wessex Poems*★ contains the masterpiece 'Drummer Hodge'. During the horror of the Great War poetry seemed inadequate so he visited the German prisoner of war Camp in Dorchester:★ one Prussian officer, in great pain, died while Hardy was with him.

**Wareham** (Anglebury). A compact town of Saxon origins surrounded still by low earth ramparts and snugly situated where the rivers Frome and Piddle enter Poole harbour. Wareham's ancient streets intersect at right angles and the town, mostly Georgian, preserves the form of a divided square. The 'Red Lion' Inn still forms a central 'angle' of the town as described in the first chapter of *The Hand of Ethelberta*,★ 'where in winter the winds whistled and assembled their forces previous to plunging helter-skelter along the streets. In summer it was a fresh and pleasant spot, convenient for such quiet characters as sojourned there to study the geology and beautiful natural features of the country around.'

Aerial view of Wareham.

**Well-Beloved, The.** First written for serialization in *Illustrated London News* from 1 October 1892 and entitled *The Pursuit of the Well-Beloved*. Hardy then wrote and published *Jude* (1895–6) before returning to revise the early chapters and rewrite the ending of *The Well-Beloved* which became Hardy's last novel to be published in book form, by Osgood, McIlvaine on 16 March 1897.

Jocelyn Pierston,★ a sculptor from the Isle of Slingers (Portland),★ pursues that 'migratory, elusive idealisation he called his Love' through three generations: Avice Caro, her daughter, and her grand-daughter. Other candidates for his fantasy are: Marcia Bencomb whom he meets by chance during a rainstorm (and while she is drying her steaming garments in a hotel where they took shelter feels that his Beloved is taking a new shape); and a high-society widow Nichola Pine-Avon, whom he visits 'with expectations of having a highly emotional time, at least'. His long trail ends with his marrying the now-aged Marcia and settling down to effect home-improvements in some Elizabethan cottages.

Despite its absurdities on the level of plot, *The Well-Beloved* is of interest as a study of the artistic temperament and offers a superb evocation of Portland ('the sea behind the pebble barrier kicked and flounced in complex rhythms, which could be translated equally well as shocks of battle or shouts of thanksgiving'). The novel's most famous admirer, Proust,★ who himself explored the theme of subjective love ('the girl whom one marries is not the person with whom one fell in love') described it as the final confirmation of the 'stone-mason's geometry' of Hardy's fiction.

No MS has survived of this novel which Hardy described as 'short and slight, and written entirely with a view to serial publication'.

**Wells, Herbert George** (1866–1946). English novelist, popularizer of 'progressive thought' and a pioneer of science-fiction. He gave an enthusiastic reception to *Jude the Obscure*★ as 'the voice of the educated proletarian, speaking more distinctly than it has ever spoken before in English literature'.

**Wessex** – see Appendix.

**'Wessex'.** A tousled brown and white Caesar terrier introduced into

Tombstone of 'Wessex' in the Max Gate pet's graveyard.

Max Gate★ by Florence Hardy★ in 1915. 'Wessex', indulged by his doting owners, became increasingly tyrannical and a menace to guests (especially at the dinner table). He died in 1926 and is buried in the Max Gate pet's cemetery. He is immortalized in the poem 'Dead "Wessex" The Dog to the Household'.

**Wessex Heights.** Though dated 1896 this magnificent and central poem was not published with Hardy's first volume of verse in 1898 (*Wessex Poems*) but held back until *Satires of Circumstance* his fourth volume, published in 1914. It was written during the fierce critical onslaught on *Jude*. Although there are several biographical references (to Florence Henniker, the 'one rare fair woman' for example) the poem exists independently of them and assumes a mythology proper to itself. The poet, depressed and lonely visits the hills of Wessex where, at least, he can know some liberty. Elsewhere he feels but a 'strange continuator' of his 'simple self that was'. Paradoxically, Hardy's description of this dispiriting state of identity crisis, imprisoned within eight bulky stanzas, is itself full of personality and life. Actor Richard Burton's excellent dramatic rendering of the poem (on Caedmon TC 1140) lifts the poem from the toils of literary detection and shows how universal this personally-inspired poem really is.

**Wessex Poems.** Hardy's first volume of verse which introduced a new phase in his literary career. It was published in December 1898 by Harper Brothers in an edition of 500 copies at 6s. with a preface and 31 illustrations by the author. Early reviewers were baffled by Hardy's changeover to verse ('We do not conceal our opinion that Mr Hardy's success in poetry is of a very narrow range ...' E. K. Chambers, *Athenaeum*, 1899). However, as a man of independent means Hardy could now pursue his first love regardless. Of the 51 poems, some of which antedate his novels, there are sufficient which speak with his unmistakable voice – 'Neutral Tones', 'Friend's Beyond',★ 'The Slow Nature'★– to announce the arrival of a major poet. The MS is in the Birmingham City Museum and Art Gallery.

**Wessex Tales.** Hardy's first collection of short stories, all of which had appeared previously in serial form, was published by Macmillan on 4 May 1888 in an edition of 750 copies at 12s. of which 634 copies were bound up and the rest remaindered. It was well-timed to follow the success of *The Woodlanders*★ and bridge the gap before the creation of *Tess*.★ These early stories are essential

Hardy – fireside tales, firmly rooted in rural tradition and legend with a relish for the eerie and the improbable. None of the stories is without its particular power but two of them – 'Fellow Towns-men,* and 'A Tradition of 1804'* – show Hardy as a supreme story-teller.

**Weymouth** (Budmouth Regis). A popular seaside town, seven miles south of Dorchester,* whose elegant Esplanade fronting the spacious bay still evokes its Georgian heyday. Here George III, the first British monarch to bathe, did so while a brass band played 'God Save the King'. Hardly lived here in 1869, at number three Wooperton Street and, perhaps in the company of Tryphena Sparks,* enjoyed 'The evening sunlit cliffs, the talk / Hailings and halts / The Morgenblatter Waltz' ('At a Seaside Town in 1896'). It occupies a central place in Wessex topography for excursions and romantic meetings. Eustacia Vye,* incarcerated on dull Egdon heath, dreamt of it constantly.

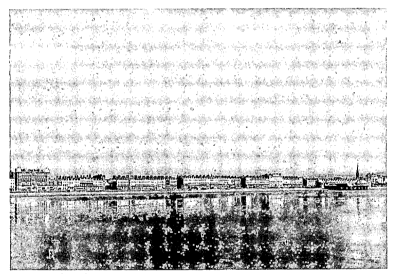

Weymouth today.

**What I Think of My Husband.** According to Florence Hardy* (letter to Clodd,* 1913), Emma Hardy assembled critical comments about her husband in her diary under this heading. Hardy dismissed them as 'sheer hallucination' and destroyed them.

**What the Shepherd Saw.** This Christmas ghost-story, seen first through the eyes of a shepherd-boy left alone to watch the flock by night on Marlbury (Malborough) Downs, appeared in *Illustrated London News* (1881) and was collected in *A Changed Man* (1913).★

**Which is the Finest View in Dorset?** Hardy's contribution to a symposium in *The Society of Dorset Men in London* (1915–16) offers eight views 'that have struck me at different times as being good'. They are noticeably panoramic (e.g. From Golden Cap, near Chideock) – as was appropriate for such a commission.

**Wildeve, Damon** (*The Return of the Native*). A handsome inn-keeper, ex-engineer, whose tendency 'to care for the remote, to dislike the near' governed his amours. After indifferently marrying Thomasin Yeobright★ he was drawn back to Eustacia Vye★ and he drowned attempting to rescue her from Shadwater weir.

**Wimborne Minster** (Warborne). A town of quiet charm dominated by its imposing but strangely coloured Minster. Hardy lived here from 1881 to 1883 at 'Llanherne', a Victorian villa with a garden full of flowers, and found the gentle social life agreeable.

**Winter Words.** Hardy's last volume of poetry, gathered at the time of his death, was published posthumously by Macmillan at 7s. 6d. in an edition of 5,000 copies on 2 October 1928. Hardy realized it was to be 'his last appearance on the literary stage'. It is a wonderful valediction with 105 poems displaying a rich variety of subject and mood: the poise of 'Lying Awake', the wit of 'Expectation and Experience', the chill of 'Standing by The Mantelpiece', the tenderness of 'The Mound'. The last poem 'He Resolves to Say No More' declares 'What I have learnt no man shall know' – an ironic statement from an artist who communicated so much.

**Winterborne, Giles** (*The Woodlanders*). A hard-working and skilful planter who 'looked and smelt like Autumn's very brother, his face being sunburnt to wheat-colour, his eyes blue as corn-flowers'. He was a man of exceptional loyalty, courage, and devotion and he died for the girl he loved.

**Winterborne Came.** A Palladian country-house (1754) overlooking rich parkland and a tiny church, hidden behind garden walls, where the poet William Barnes★ was rector. The thatched rectory stands nearby on the Dorchester★–Wareham★ road. One of Hardy's favourite walks led from Max Gate★ through the park to Winterborne Came church.

**Withered Arm, The.** A macabre story of witchcraft based on a belief which still persists in Dorset★ in 'the turn o' the blood'.

William Barnes' thatched rectory.

Rhoda Brook curses Gertrude Lodge, the girl who had supplanted her in the affections of Farmer Lodge. Gertrude's arm begins to wither and she turns to superstition and magic for a cure, agreeing to touch the neck of a freshly hanged man. The victim for her ordeal turns out to be her husband's illegitimate son and she dies from the shock three days later. The story was first printed in *Blackwood's Edinburgh Magazine* in 1888 and later collected in *Wessex Tales* (1888).★

**Without Ceremony.** One of the simplest and most poignant of the *Poems 1912–13*.★ Hardy's recollection of Emma's★ unsociable habit of departing 'without a word' manages, within its three verses, to combine the greatest possible number of reflections on his wife's strange ways.

**Women.** Hardy experienced intense feelings for women all his life – from his childhood attachment to the lady of the manor (Julia Augusta Martin★) to his octogenarian admiration for a beautiful young actress (Gertrude Bugler★). His gallery of fictional women, intuitively known, presents them warmly and sensually (e.g. Eustacia Vye's★ mouth 'formed less to speak than to quiver, less to quiver than to kiss'); glimpsed in feminine poses (e.g. Bathsheba Everdene★ smiling into her small swing-mirror); in diverse roles – queen, temptress, mother, mistress, flirt, gossip, victim; from all

175

rungs of the social ladder. As well as young and fateful heroines the gallery contains old crones and witches (e.g. Susan Nunsuch★), buxom matrons and gossips (e.g. Mother Cuxsom★) and common beauties (e.g. Izzy Huett★).

He explores the paradox of woman's weakness and vulnerability co-existing with great strength based on closeness to life and their own feelings. Beside negative statements such as: 'Time and circumstance, which enlarge the views of most men narrow the views of women almost invariably' (*Jude*★) or 'Succeeding generations of women are seldom marked by cumulative progress, their advance as girls being lost in their recession as matrons' – (*The Well-Beloved*),★ there are those countless celebrations of feminine beauty, intuition, charm, strength, creativity and eternal attractiveness culminating in his lyrical and almost lover-like portrayal of Tess,★ his favourite woman.

'In the Hardy Gallery' by A. G. McFadden.

Hardy placed more emphasis on their fatality but this was inevitable for characters central to a writer of fundamentally tragic vision. Hardy's women are the embodiment of doomed rural England, their lushness, fertility, and frail loveliness threatened by the unnatural progress of civilization.

'It seems as if, in delineating the sufferings of Bathsheba, Tess, and Sue, Hardy succeeded in tapping the vein of trembling wondering love which had originated in him as a child, which had come to fulfilment in his love of Emma Lavinia, and which, though it by-passed her, never ceased to quiver and function' (Rosalind Miles 'The Women of Wessex', *The Novels of Thomas Hardy*, 1979).

**Woodlanders, The.** Originally alternatively entitled *Fitzpiers at Hintock*, it was written at Max Gate in 1885–7 and based on a 'woodland story' Hardy had conceived about ten years earlier. It was serialized in *Macmillans Magazine* and *Harpers Bazaar* from May 1886 to April 1887 and published by Macmillan in a three-volume edition of 1,000 copies at 31s. 6d. on 15 March 1887. It was a considerable success and Hardy later regarded it as in some respects his best novel.

It combines the pastoral★ simplicity of earlier novels with a more impressionistic technique. The sequestered woodlands of Little Hintock witness the converging destinies of five characters: Giles Winterborne★ and Marty South★ (natural woodlanders); Grace Melbury★ (a woodlander educated elsewhere); Mrs Charmond★ and Dr Fitzpiers★ (outsiders with alien values). Their misfortunes and mis-matchings are seen in both comic and tragic perspectives. Detailed descriptions of the woodland landscape ('trunks with spreading roots whose mossed rinds made them like hands wearing green gloves elbowed old elms and ashes with great forks, in which stood pools of water that overflowed on rainy days, and ran down their stems in green cascades') give *The Woodlanders* a static and pictorial effect. Within this firmly delivered natural setting the characters are microscopically examined as though in a laboratory and the novel's open ending confirms our sense of their separateness. Mrs Charmond is dead and Grace Melbury has settled for a convenient reunion with her husband Fitzpiers; Marty South lays flowers on the grave of Giles Winterborne declaring, 'I never can forget 'ee; for you was a good man and did good things!'

Hardy inscribed copies of *The Woodlanders* to Gosse★ and Swinburne.★ The MS is in the Dorset County Museum.

Woolbridge Manor.

**Woolbridge Manor** (Wellbridge Manor). A mellow stone and brick Elizabethan house standing dramatically alone by the river Frome (Froom) where Tess★ spent her wretched honeymoon. Hermann Lea★ noted that 'of all the scenes which occur throughout the Wessex★ novels no place is so near to reality or so familiar to my readers as this house'. It is now a hotel.

**Woolf, Virginia** (1882–1941). Leslie Stephen's youngest daughter, Virginia, married Leonard Woolf (1880–1969) in 1912. He encouraged her brilliant but unstable literary life which ended with her suicide on 28 March 1941. She achieved fame as an experimental novelist who sought to capture the living moment but her *Collected Essays* (1966) and *Diaries* (being published in five volumes) may prove her greatest achievements. Her special feeling for Hardy informs her essay *The Novels of Thomas Hardy* in which she refers to 'the margin of the unexpressed' in them. She visited Max Gate★ on 25 July 1926 and found Hardy 'loathe to talk about writing' but showing, 'freedom, ease, and vitality. He seemed very "Great Victorian" doing the whole thing with a sweep of his hand' (Diary).

Virginia Woolf.

**Wordsworth, William** (1770–1850). A revolutionary poet whose extreme romantic self-consciousness discovered a relationship with the external world. Hardy, during a time of 'mental depression over his work and prospects', noted in July 1868 that reading Wordsworth's *Resolution and Independence* was a cure for despair. During better times in the summer of 1873 he and Emma Gifford★ visited Tintern Abbey ('a wooded slope visible from every mullioned window') where they spoke some lines of Wordsworth and afterwards absorbed the silence of the place.

# Y

**Yeats, William Butler** (1865–1939). Twentieth-century Irish lyric poet who adopted different 'masks' for the phases of his development. On 1 June 1912 he presented Hardy with the Royal Society of Literature's gold medal.

179

**Yellow-Hammer, The.** In this uncollected poem Hardy describes how yellow-hammers pursue the heavily-laden harvest waggons along the dry summer lanes 'seize a wheat-ear by the stem / And are gone...'

**Yeobright, Clym** (*The Return of the Native*). After an early education he left his native Egdon heath★ (being a lad 'of whom something was expected'), worked for a time in Budmouth and London (like Hardy) and began a promising career in Paris in the diamond business. His self-absorbed, serious-minded idealism led him back home to seek a more worthwhile life. Against his own better judgement and his possessive mother's wishes he married the restless Eustacia Vye★ who regarded his beloved heath as a prison. Their disastrous marriage became a scene of bitter quarrelling and recrimination leading to complete breakdown. Mrs Yeobright died on a mission of reconciliation and Clym, racked by guilt and remorse, turned his fury on Eustacia. She drowned in a confused attempt to leave Egdon with a former lover and Clym, feeling responsible for the death of the two women who had meant most to him, became an itinerant preacher 'on morally unimpeachable themes'.

**Yeobright, Mrs** (*The Return of the Native*). A strong-willed, possessive mother whose own disappointments made her ambitious for her son, Clym,★ and her niece, Thomasin.★ After her niece is brought home humiliated by the cancellation of her marriage (through some obscure hitch) she maintains calm until Thomasin's faithful friend Diggory Venn★ is out of hearing. 'Now Thomasin,' she said sternly, 'what's the meaning of this disgraceful performance?' Her confrontations with Clym over his career and choice of wife surge from equally deep sources of resentment. Hardy presents her viewpoint compassionately and as she lay exhausted on the heath, 'a broken-hearted woman cast off by her son', she watches a heron take flight 'away from the earthly ball to which she was pinioned ... But, being a mother, it was inevitable that she should soon cease to ruminate upon her own condition.' She is one of Hardy's most singular creations.

**Yeobright, Thomasin** (*The Return of the Native*). A simple girl with 'a fair, sweet and honest country face'. She sets off alone for her marriage to the selfish Damon Wildeve★ watched by Mrs Yeobright★ who sees, 'a little figure wending its way between the scratching furze-bushes, and diminishing far up the valley – a pale

blue spot in a vast field of neutral brown, solitary and undefended
except by the power of her own hope'. Throughout the novel she is
loved from afar by a strange, loyal admirer called Diggory Venn.★
One of the few joyful events in this tragic novel is her marriage to
him at the end.

# HARDY'S WESSEX

Nearly every place in Hardy's fiction has a real counterpart in a large area of Southern and Western England from Hampshire to Cornwall. Hardy divided it into North Wessex (Berkshire), Mid-Wessex (Wiltshire), Upper Wessex (Hampshire), Outer Wessex (Somerset), South Wessex (Dorset), Lower Wessex (Devon), and Off-Wessex (Cornwall). South Wessex is the heart of the region.

Hardy adopted the name 'Wessex', first used in *Far From the Madding Crowd*, from the ancient West Saxon kingdom. The now-familiar names of Wessex places were gradually evolved. There is controversy over the identification of some of them but most can be definitely located – from Hardy's identification, the names themselves (e.g. Abbot's Cernel for Cerne Abbas), topographical features reflected in the names, historical association, detection by literary pilgrims.

In the 1895 Preface to *Tess of the D'Urbervilles*, Hardy wrote, 'It may be wise to state clearly at the outset that the author has never admitted more than that the places named fictitiously were *suggested* by such and such real places. But assuming these places of fiction and verse to be idealizations, there is little difficulty in recognizing the majority of them in substance.' This established an important principle of relationship between Casterbridge and Dorchester.

Hardy discovered himself as a novelist by exploiting his exceptionally strong sense of place for a deeper purpose. He translated personal and intractable material into parable and was able to preserve both his privacy and his artistic freedom. Wessex, Hardy's 'partly real, partly dream-country' in which he was both observer and participant, remains essentially fictional.

Melvyn Bragg has suggested, in an essay *Thomas Hardy and Jude the Obscure* (Budmouth Essays, 1976), that the invasion of Hardy's personal experiences into his final novels, *Jude the Obscure* especially, led to the disintegration of Wessex and his abandonment of the novel. 'In *Jude* . . . he saw that the things inside him could get out in ways which disturbed his sense of secrecy, propriety, and perhaps even survival.' But his fictional kingdom had been created and is one of the great achievements of modern literature.

Recommended books dealing with topography:

*The History and Antiquities of the County of Dorset*, John Hutchins (1774). It was Hardy's principal source.
*The Wessex of Thomas Hardy*, B. C. A. Windle, illustrated by E. H. New (1902).
*Thomas Hardy's Wessex*, Hermann Lea (1913).
*A Hardy Companion*, F. B. Pinion (1968).
*Hardy's Wessex Re-Appraised*, Denys Kay-Robinson (1972).
*Discovering Hardy's Wessex*, Anne-Marie Edwards (1978). Describes walks in Wessex with excellent maps and commentary.

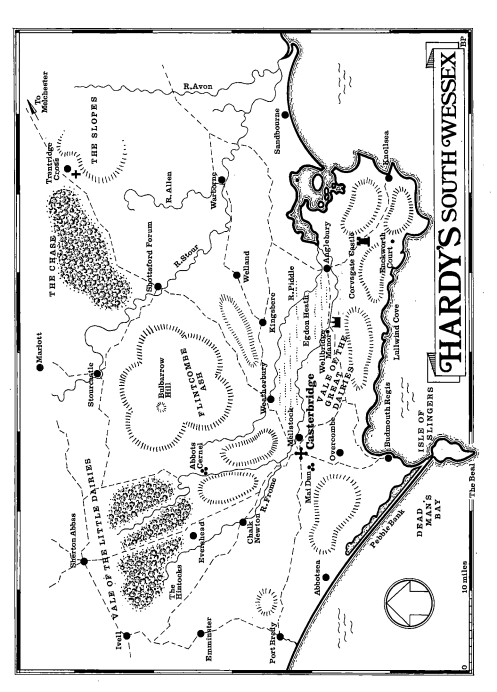

HARDY'S SOUTH WESSEX

| *Wessex Place Names* | *Geographical Place Names* |
|---|---|
| Abbot's Cernel | Cerne Abbas. |
| Abbotsea | Abbotsbury – A village with a long street of yellowstone and thatched cottages, a large tithe-barn built by monks who also established a famous swannery. Nearby White Hill commands a magnificent view above Abbotsbury's sub-tropical gardens of the 500-year-old stone-roofed Chapel of St Catherine with the vast sweep of Chesil Beach beyond. |
| Aldbrickham | Reading (Berkshire). |
| Alderworth | A lonely cottage surrounded by firs near Affpuddle. |
| Alfredston | Wantage (Berkshire). |
| Anglebury | Wareham. |
| Arrowthorne Lodge | Difficult to establish, most likely position is Breamore House, north of Fording-bridge. |
| Aquae Sulis | Bath (Somerset), featured in a poem of that title. Elsewhere Hardy uses the real name |

Cerne Abbas.

|  |  |
|---|---|
|  | for Bath. The poem 'Midnight on Beechen, 187–' evokes 'Bath's dim concave, towers, and spire' on his visit to Emma Lavinia Gifford in June 1873. |
| Athelhall | Athelhampton Manor, east of Puddletown. |
| Barwith Strand | Trebarwith Strand (Cornwall). |
| Batton Castle | Difficult to establish. Possibly Badminton House near Castle Combe (Wiltshire). |
| Beal, The | Portland Bill. Famous headland from which Anne Garland watched H.M.S. *Victory* sail past, a great, silent ship with the aspect 'of a large white bat'. |
| Beeny Cliff | Beeny High Cliff (Cornwall). |
| Blackmoor, or Blackmore Vale | Valley to the north of Sturminster Newton which Hardy extended to cover a wider area of undulating wooded country. See Valley of the Little Dairies. |
| Black'on | Blackdown Hill, a National Trust property three miles north-east of Abbotsbury which is topped by a stone pillar commemorating Admiral Hardy. |
| Bloom's-End | A valley south of Rushy-Pond. 'Bloom's-End' house of *The Return of the Native* cannot be precisely located. |
| Bramshurst Manor-House | Moyle's Court, near Ringwood (Hampshire). |
| Broad Sidlinch | Sydling St Nicholas. |
| Budmouth Regis | Weymouth. |
| Camelton | Camelford (Cornwall). |
| Carriford | An imaginary village suggested by parts of West Stafford. |
| Casterbridge | Dorchester. |
| Castle Boterel | Boscastle. |
| Castle Royal | Windsor Castle (Berkshire). |
| Chalk-Newton | Maiden-Newton. |
| Chaseborough | Cranborne Chase. |
| Chesil Bank (or Pebble Bank) | Chesil Beach. A long reef extending 16 miles from Portland to Abbotsbury covered with an immense wall of shingle |

piled high by stormy seas and strong currents. The pebbles increase in size going westwards, and enabled smugglers to locate their exact position in darkness. The Iron Age defenders of Maiden Castle used the pebbles for ammunition. The great gale of November 1874 (mentioned in *The Woodlanders*) blew a ship right over the bank into the Fleet.

| | |
|---|---|
| Christminster | Oxford. |
| Cliff Without a Name | Beeny High Cliff. |
| Corvsgate Castle | Corfe Castle. |
| Cresscombe | Letcombe Bassett (Berkshire). |
| Creston | Preston, north of Weymouth. |
| Cross-in-Hand | A mysterious stone pillar (known locally as 'Crossy-Hand') standing in roadside grass at nearly the highest point of Batcombe Down. |
| Damer's Wood | Came Wood, two miles south of Dorchester. |
| Deadman's Bay | Lyme and West Bays. Well named 'Deadman's Bay' for 'if a vessel once gets inside it during a gale there is ... a practical certainty of its being dashed to pieces on the beach' (Hermann Lea). In *The Well-Beloved* Hardy describes the huge composite ghost of shipwrecked-victims who have 'rolled each other to oneness on that restless seabed'. |
| Downstaple | Barnstaple (Devon). |
| Dundagel | Tintagel (Cornwall). |
| Durnover | Fordington (Dorchester). The name derives from the Roman name 'Durnovaria'. Hardy's great friend Horace Moule's father was rector at Fordingham. |
| East Egdon | Affpuddle. |
| East Endelstow | Lesnewth (Cornwall). |
| East Quarries | Easton, Portland. |
| East Mellstock | Lower Bockhampton. |

Egdon Heath

An amalgam of heathlands and forestry stretching eastwards from Stinsford to the north of Poole Harbour. 'Under the general name of "Egdon Heath" ... are united or typified heaths of various real names, to the number of at least a dozen ...'. Despite its sombre character, the heath is 'a spot which returned upon the memory of those who loved it ...'

Eggar

Eggardon Hill.

Emminster

Beaminster.

Endelstow

St Juliot.

Eggardon.

Endelstow House

Modelled on Lanhydrock House, near Bodmin (Cornwall).

Enckworth Court

Encombe House, set deeply in a beautiful valley running down to the sea between Kimmeridge Bay and Chapman's Pool and backed by a steep ridge of the Purbeck Hills.

Evershead

Evershot, 12 miles north-west of Dorchester.

Encombe House.

| | |
|---|---|
| Exonbury | Exeter (Devon). |
| Flintcomb-Ash | Difficult to locate exactly in a wide area between Abbot's Cernel and Shottsford-Forum. The many suggestions by topographers include Barcombe Down, near Alton Pancras, Nettlecombe-Tout, Plush, and Dole's Ash Farm. It is a supreme example of Hardy's allegorical use of landscape to express a state of mind; during Tess's desolate period at Flintcomb-Ash 'the unforgiving landscape is as stripped of comfort and vegetation as she is of love and hope'. |
| Flychett | Lychett Minster, five miles east of Wareham. |
| Founthall | Wells (Somerset). Named from the springs which flow from the Mendip Hills. |
| Froom, The | River Frome, which runs through the heart of South Wessex past Dorchester and Woolbridge Manor into Poole Harbour, near Wareham. cf. 'The Slow Nature'. |

| | |
|---|---|
| Froom–Everard | West Stafford House. |
| Froom–Side Vale | Frome Valley: see Valley of the Great Dairies. |
| Glaston | Glastonbury (Somerset). |
| Gloucester Lodge | Gloucester Hotel, Weymouth. |
| Great Forest | The New Forest (Hampshire). |
| Great Hintock | See The Hintocks. |
| Great Plain, The | Salisbury Plain (Wiltshire). |
| Greenhill | Woodbury Hill, near Bere Regis. |
| Grey's Bridge | Bridge on the A35 road just on the edge of Dorchester. |
| Grey's Wood | North of the Dorchester–Puddletown road. Dick Dewy went nutting here when he was tired of waiting for Fancy Day. |
| Haggardon Hill | Eggardon Hill. Steep hill five miles north-east of Bridport crowned with a prehistoric camp. |
| Havenpool | Poole. |
| Henry VIII's Castle | Sandsfoot Castle, Weymouth. |
| High Place Hall | Colliton House, Dorchester. |
| Hintock House | Turnworth House (now demolished). |
| Hintocks, The | 'The most elusive of landscapes in the greater novels' (Denys Kay-Robinson). Hardy changed the location from Melbury Osmond/Bubb Down region to High Stoy and Minterne Magna about four miles to the east. |
| Holmstoke | Based on East Stoke, near Wareham. |
| Idmouth | Sidmouth (Devon). |
| Isle of Slingers | Portland. |
| Ivelchester | Ilchester (Somerset). |
| Ivell | Yeovil (Somerset). |
| Kennetbridge | Newbury, on the River Kennet (Berkshire). |
| Kingbere | Bere Regis. |
| King's Hintock | Melbury Osmond. |
| Knapwater House | Kingston Maurward. |
| Knollsea | Swanage. |
| Leddenton | Gillingham (named from the River Lodden). |

Kingston Maurward.

| | |
|---|---|
| Little Enckworth | Kingston, two miles south of Corfe Castle. |
| Longpuddle | A disputed place, suggested by the long valley of the Piddle (or Puddle) river which runs through the villages of Piddletren-thide and Piddlehinton. It is sometimes called Upper or Lower Longpuddle. |
| Lower Mellstock | Lower Bockhampton. |
| Lulwind (or Lulstead) Cove | Lulworth Cove, where the chalk cliffs reach out symmetrically to encircle a lake-like body of water. Its spectacular beauty is best appreciated out of the tourist season. cf. 'At Lulworth Cove a Century Back.' |
| Mai-Dun (or Maidon) Castle | Maiden Castle. |
| Markton | Dunster (Somerset). |
| Marlbury Downs | Marlborough Downs (Wiltshire). |
| Marlott | Marnhull. |
| Marygreen | Great Fawley (Berkshire). |
| Melchester | Salisbury. |
| Mellstock | Stinsford. |
| Middleton Abbey | Milton Abbas. |
| Mistover Knap | Somewhere north of Rainbarrows. |

Looking towards Lulworth Cove.

Stinsford. One of Hardy's favourite walks, from Stinsford to Lower Bockhampton.

| | |
|---|---|
| Mixen Lane | Mill Street, Fordington. |
| Moreford Rise | A hill near Moreton village. |
| Narrobourne | West Coker (Somerset). |
| Nether Moynton | Overmoigne. |
| Newland Buckton | Buckland Newton. |
| Norcombe Hill | Disputed. Most likely drawn from Toller Down north-east of Beaminster. Hardy's description of a 'featureless convexity of chalk and soil ... which may remain undisturbed on some great day of confusion when far grander heights ... topple down' could apply to many hills, in the area north of Bridport. |
| Nuttlebury | Hazelbury Bryan. |
| Oakbury Fitzpiers | Okeford Fitzpaine. |
| Old Melchester | Old Sarum (Wiltshire). |
| Overcombe | A village suggested mainly by Sutton Poyntz but the church is that at Bincombe, a tiny and remote place below the downs. |
| Owlscombe | Batcombe. |
| Oxwell Hall | Poxwell Hall. |
| Pen–Zepher | Penzance (Cornwall). |
| Port–Bredy | Bridport. |
| Po'sham | Portisham. |
| Quartershot | Aldershot. |
| Rainbarrow | Rainbarrows, burial mounds north of the Dorchester–Wareham road on high heathland, where we are first introduced to Eustacia Vye, 'above the hill rose the barrow, and above the barrow rose the figure ...' |
| Ridgeway | Ancient way over the downs between Dorchester and Weymouth. |
| Ring, The | Maumbury Rings, just outside Dorchester on the Weymouth road. Once solitary and sinister, it is now hemmed in by railways. |
| Roytown | Troytown, a small hamlet west of Puddletown. |
| Rushy–Pond | A pool on Puddletown heath where old roads meet. |
| Sandbourne | Bournemouth (Hampshire). |

| | |
|---|---|
| Scrimpton | Frampton. |
| Shadwater Weir (the Great Pool) | Sturt's Weir, near Woodsford. |
| Shaston | Shaftesbury. |
| Sherton Abbas | Sherborne. |
| Shottsford Forum | Blandford Forum. |
| Solentsea | Southsea. |
| St Launce's | Launceston (Cornwall). |
| Stancy Castle | Modelled on Dunster Castle (Somerset). |
| Stapleford | Stalbridge. |
| Stickleford | Tincleton, village four miles east of Dorchester. |
| Stoke-Barehills | Basingstoke. |
| Stourcastle | Sturminster Newton. |
| Street of Wells | Fortuneswell, Portland. |

Tincleton.

| | |
|---|---|
| Sylvania Castle | Pennsylvania Castle, Portland, built for John Penn, grandson of William Penn, the founder of Pennsylvania, is an unusual castellated pastiche of styles. It is now an eleg- |

ant hotel surrounded by trees command-
ing fine sea views.

Talbothays — A typical Frome-Valley dairy-farm whose
location is disputed. The name derives
from a farm owned by Hardy's father near
West Stafford.

Pennsylvania Castle.

| | |
|---|---|
| Targan Bay | Pentargan Bay (Cornwall). |
| Tolchurch | Tolpuddle. |
| Toneborough | Taunton (Somerset). |
| Tor-Upon-Sea | Torquay (Devon). |
| Trantridge | Based on both Pentridge, near Cranborne, and Tarrant Hinton, near Blandford. |
| Trufoe | Truro (Cornwall). |
| Upper Mellstock | Higher Bockhampton. |
| Vale of the Great Dairies | Frome Valley. |
| Vale of the Little Dairies | Blackmoor Vale. |

195

| | |
|---|---|
| Warborne | Wimborne Minster. |
| Weatherbury | Puddletown. |
| Weatherbury Farm | Based on Waterstone Manor (one and a half miles west of Puddletown). |
| Welland House | Suggested by Charborough House. |
| Wellbridge Abbey | Bindon Abbey. |
| Wellbridge Manor | Woolbridge Manor, near Wool. |
| Wessex Heights | Ingpen Beacon, Wylls Neck, Bulbarrow, Pilsdon. |
| West Endelstow | St Juliot. |
| West Mellstock | Stinsford. |
| Weydon Priors | Weyhill (Hampshire). |
| Wintoncester | Winchester. |
| Yalbury (or Yell'ham) Wood | Yellowham Wood, between Dorchester and Puddletown. Joseph Poorgrass, stopping the waggon which bore Fanny Robin's coffin through the wood, 'listened. Not a footstep or wheel was audible anywhere around, and the dead silence was broken only by a heavy particle falling from a tree through the evergreens and alighting with a smart rap upon the coffin of poor Fanny'. |

# CHRONOLOGY: THOMAS HARDY
## 1840–1928

1840     Born at Higher Bockhampton, Dorset, on 2 June, eldest child of Thomas and Jemima (Hand) Hardy.

1848     Goes to village school at Lower Bockhampton established by Julia Augusta Martin, lady of Kingston Maurward manor.

1849     Goes to school in Dorchester. Plays fiddle at local dances and weddings. Avid reader.

1856–61 Articled to Dorchester architect, John Hicks. Contact with Dorset poet William Barnes. Studies Greek with the assistance of Horace Moule, his elder friend and mentor. Writes poetry. Witnesses public execution. 'three-fold life' – professional, scholarly, rustic.

1862–7 Goes to London and works as assistant architect to Arthur Blomfield. Takes great interest in the cultural life of the capital. Extensive reading in modern poetry and 'advanced thinkers'. Poems rejected by periodicals. Becomes agnostic.

1867     Returns home to Dorset because of ill-health to work for Hicks again.

1868     Completes *The Poor Man and the Lady* (unpublished).

1869     In Weymouth working for architect G. R. Crickmay. Possible emotional involvement with Tryphena Sparks.

1870     Sent by Crickmay to St Juliot, Cornwall to examine church. Meets future wife Emma Lavinia Gifford. Excursions to Boscastle, Tintagel, and Beeny Cliff.

1871     *Desperate Remedies* published on 25 March. Visits to Cornwall. Miss Gifford encourages him to persevere with novel writing.

1872     *Under the Greenwood Tree* favourably received, 'with the genuine air of the country breathing throughout it'. Working in London again. Emma's father disapproves of Hardy.

1873     *A Pair of Blue Eyes*. Invited by Leslie Stephen to write a

Hardy's statue, Dorchester.

serial for Cornhill Magazine. Horace Moule commits suicide 21 September. Hardy begins writing his new novel at
the family home in Higher Bockhampton.

1874 Marries Emma Gifford on 17 September at St Peter's

Emma Lavinia
Gifford at St Juliot.

church, Paddington. Honeymoon on the continent. The Hardys take rooms at St David's Villa, Hook Road, Surbiton. *Far From the Madding Crowd* an immediate success.

1875    The Hardys move house three times within a year at London, Swanage, and Yeovil. Hardy writing novel with change of theme and background.

1876    *The Hand of Ethelberta* published on 3 April. Tour to Holland and the Rhine Valley. Move into the first house they had to themselves, Riverside Villa, Sturminster Newton, Dorset. 'Our happiest time'. Writes *The Return of the Native.*

1878    Moves back to London, for its professional facilities, to 1 Arundel Terrace, Trinity Road, Upper Tooting. Joins Savile Club and enters literary and social circles.

1880    *The Trumpet-Major* published on 26 October. Returns from a tour in France and is immobilized by serious illness while writing *A Laodicean*. Dictated rest of novel to Emma.

# Chronology

Thrush') printed in the *Graphic*, 29 December 1900. 'And every spirit upon earth / Seemed fervourless as I'.

1901   *Poems of the Past and Present*, an instant success, established Hardy as poet in his own right. Begins work on a massive poetic conception he had nourished for years. *The Dynasts*.

1904   Death of Hardy's mother on 3 April.

1907   Emma Hardy walks in a procession of suffragettes in London. Hardy meets Florence Emily Dugdale.

1908   *The Dynasts* completed. Edits selection from the poems of William Barnes.

1909   Declines invitation to USA. Becomes governor of Dorchester Grammar School, President of the Society of Authors. *Time's Laughingstocks*.

1910   Receives Order of Merit, and the freedom of Dorchester.

1912   First two volumes of Wessex Edition of his novels published. Suddenly, unexpectedly, Emma Hardy died on 27 November. Hardy overwhelmed with grief and remorse.

1913   Hardy makes pilgrimage to St Juliot. Begins writing a flood of poems about Emma and their romance. *A Changed Man and Other Tales*.

1914   Marries Florence Emily Dugdale at St Andrew's Church, Enfield, on 10 February. Outbreak of the war. Hardy joins group of writers pledged to write for the Allied Cause. *Satires of Circumstance* (including *Poems 1912–13*) published 17 November.

1915   Death of Hardy's sister Mary.

1917   *Moments of Vision*. Hardy increasingly withdrawn, shut up in his study, evolving intense personal mythology. Florence Hardy suffers depressions. Hardy and Florence begin work on *The Life*.

1920   Bathroom with hot water installed at Max Gate. Hardy receives honorary D.Litt. from Oxford. Last visit to London.

1922   *Late Lyrics and Earlier*. Hardy rebuts charges of pessimism. Enjoys motoring. Visits Stinsford, 'sunshine, mist and turning leaves'.

1923   *The Famous Tragedy of the Queen of Cornwall*. The Prince of Wales received at Max Gate. Telephone installed.

1924   Florence enters London Nursing home for operation.

1925   *Human Shows, Far Phantasies, Songs*, and *Trifles*.

## Chronology

1926    Virginia Woolf visits Max Gate which had been receiving increasing numbers of young writers and poets. Hardy visits his birthplace for the last time. Death of the Hardys' famous dog 'Wessex'. Hardy did not sit up for New Year's Eve.

1927    Last public appearance: Address at Dorchester Grammar School stone-laying. In November visits Stinsford to put flowers on family graves. Hardy continues writing and revising poems. He recalls how when he was a child he used to go on his hands and knees and pretend to eat grass to see what the sheep would do. Final illness begins in December.

1928    On 10 January insists on writing cheque for the Pension Fund of the Society of Authors. On the evening of 11 January dies at Max Gate. *Winter Words* published posthumously.

# THE CHARACTERS OF HARDY'S NOVELS

## A Selective Finding List

### A

| | |
|---|---|
| Aldclyffe, Captain Gerald Fellcourt | *Desperate Remedies* |
| Aldclyffe, Miss Cytherea | *Desperate Remedies* |
| Aldritch, Dr | *Far From the Madding Crowd* |
| Anny | *Jude the Obscure* |
| Atway, Mrs | *The Well-Beloved* |

### B

| | |
|---|---|
| Baker, Farmer | *Desperate Remedies* |
| Ball, Abel | *Far From the Madding Crowd* |
| Barker, Dr | *Far From the Madding Crowd* |
| Barret, Sam | *The Woodlanders* |
| Bates, Grammer | *A Pair of Blue Eyes* |
| Bath, Dr | *Mayor of Casterbridge* |
| Bath, Mrs | *Mayor of Casterbridge* |
| Beach, Esther | *The Trumpet-Major* |
| Beaucock, Fred | *The Woodlanders* |
| Belinda | *Jude the Obscure* |
| Bell, Barbara | *A Laodicean* |
| Belmaine, Miss | *The Hand of Ethelberta* |
| Belmaine, Mrs | *The Hand of Ethelberta* |
| Bencombe, Marcia | *The Well-Beloved* |
| Bencombe, Mr | *The Well-Beloved* |
| Bicknell, Miss | *A Pair of Blue Eyes* |
| Biles, 'Hezzy' | *Two on a Tower* |
| Billet, Dairyman | *Tess of the D'Urbervilles* |
| Birch, Milly | *A Laodicean* |
| Blandsbury, Sir Cyril and Lady | *The Hand of Ethelberta* |
| Blore, Sammy | *Two on a Tower* |
| Blowbody, Mrs | *The Mayor of Casterbridge* |
| Boldwood, Farmer | *Far From the Madding Crowd* |
| Boldwood, Farmer | *The Mayor of Casterbridge* |
| Bollen, Farmer | *The Woodlanders* |

## Characters

## C

| | |
|---|---|
| Chancerley, Mr | *The Hand of Ethelberta* |
| Changly, Jack | *The Return of the Native* |
| Channelcliffe, Countess and Earl of | *The Well-Beloved* |
| Chant, Mercy | *Tess of the D'Urbervilles* |
| Chapman, Nathaniel | *Two on a Tower* |
| Charl | *The Mayor of Casterbridge* |
| Charley | *The Return of the Native* |
| Charmond, Mrs Felice | *The Woodlanders* |
| Chestman, Dr | *Desperate Remedies* |
| Chickerel, Ethelberta | *The Hand of Ethelberta* |
| Chickerels, The – Cornelia, Dan, Georgina, Gwendoline, Joseph, Mr, Mrs, Myrtle, Picotee, Sol | *The Hand of Ethelberta* |
| Chinny, Joseph | *Desperate Remedies* |
| Clare, Angel | *Tess of the D'Urbervilles* |
| Clares, The – Cuthbert, Felix, Mrs, Rev. James | *Tess of the D'Urbervilles* |
| Clark, Mark | *Far From the Madding Crowd* |
| Claydonfield, Lord | *Desperate Remedies* |
| Cockman | *Jude the Obscure* |
| Coggans, The – Bob, Charlotte, Jan, Mrs, Teddy | *Far From the Madding Crowd* |
| Comfort, James and his wife | *The Trumpet-Major* |
| Coney, Christopher | *The Mayor of Casterbridge* |
| Constantine, Lady Viviette | *Two on a Tower* |
| Constantine, Sir Blount | *Two on a Tower* |
| Coole, Mr | *A Pair of Blue Eyes* |
| Cormick, Old James and son | *The Trumpet-Major* |
| Cox, Mrs | *The Woodlanders* |
| Creedle, Robert | *The Woodlanders* |
| Crick, Dairyman and his wife | *Tess of the D'Urbervilles* |
| Crickett, Richard and his wife | *Desperate Remedies* |
| Cripplestraw, Anthony | *The Trumpet-Major* |
| Crumpler, Simon and his wife | *Under the Greenwood Tree* |
| Cunningham, Captain | *The Trumpet-Major* |
| Cuxsom, Mother | *The Mayor of Casterbridge* |

## D

| | |
|---|---|
| Damson, Suke | *The Woodlanders* |
| Darch, Car | *Tess of the D'Urbervilles* |
| Darch, Nancy | *Tess of the D'Urbervilles* |
| Dare, William | *A Laodicean* |
| Day, Fancy | *Under the Greenwood Tree* |
| Days, Geoffrey, Jane | *Under the Greenwood Tree* |
| Day, John | *Desperate Remedies* |
| Derriman, Benjamin (Old Benjy) and his nephew Festus | *The Trumpet-Major* |
| De Stancy, Charlotte | *A Laodicean* |
| De Stancys, The Captain, Sir William | *A Laodicean* |
| Deverell, Miss | *A Laodicean* |
| Dewy, Dick | *Under the Greenwood Tree* |
| Dewys, The – Bessy, Bob, Charley Jimmy, Mrs Ann, Reuben, Susan, 'Grandfather' William | *Under the Greenwood Tree* |
| Dickson, Mr | *Desperate Remedies* |
| Dodman, Dairyman | *Desperate Remedies* |
| Dollery, Mrs | *The Woodlanders* |
| Dollop, Jack | *Tess of the D'Urbervilles* |
| Doncastle, Mr and Mrs | *The Hand of Ethelberta* |
| Donns, The – Mr, Mrs and Arabella | *Jude the Obscure* |
| Dowden, Olly | *The Return of the Native* |
| Dummett, Joan | *The Mayor of Casterbridge* |
| D'Urberville, Alec, his mother | *Tess of the D'Urbervilles* |
| Durbeyfield, Tess | *Tess of the D'Urbervilles* |
| Durbeyfields, The – Abraham, Hope, Joan, John, Liza-Lu, Modesty, Sorrow | *Tess of the D'Urbervilles* |
| Durford, John | *Under the Greenwood Tree* |

## E

| | |
|---|---|
| Edlin, Mrs | *Jude the Obscure* |
| Egloskerry, Mr | *A Pair of Blue Eyes* |
| Ellis, Miss | *The Woodlanders* |

**Characters**

## K

| | |
|---|---|
| Kail, Jonathan | *Tess of the D'Urbervilles* |
| Kayte, Grammer | *Under the Greenwood Tree* |
| Kex, Farmer | *Under the Greenwood Tree* |
| Kibbs, Captain Job and his wife | *The Well-Beloved* |
| Kingsmore, Arthur | *A Pair of Blue Eyes* |
| Knibbs, Beck | *Tess of the D'Urbervilles* |
| Knight, Henry | *A Pair of Blue Eyes* |

## L

| | |
|---|---|
| Ladywell | *The Hand of Ethelberta* |
| Lark, Tabitha | *Two on a Tower* |
| Lawson, Sam | *Under the Greenwood Tree* |
| Leafs, The – Mr, Mrs, Thomas | *Under the Greenwood Tree* |
| Leat, Mrs Elizabeth | *Desperate Remedies* |
| Ledlow, Farmer and his wife | *Under the Greenwood Tree* |
| Leverre, Henri | *The Well-Beloved* |
| Lickpans, The – Joseph, Levi, Robert | *A Pair of Blue Eyes* |
| Little Father Time | *Jude the Obscure* |
| Long, Lawyer | *Far From the Madding Crowd* |
| Longway, Solomon | *The Mayor of Casterbridge* |
| Lovedays, The – Miller Loveday, John, Bob | *The Trumpet-Major* |
| Luxellians, The – Lord Spenser Hugo, Lord George, Lady Elfride, Kate, Mary | *A Pair of Blue Eyes* |

## M

| | |
|---|---|
| Mail, Michael | *Under the Greenwood Tree* |
| Manstons, The – Mrs Manston, Aeneas, Eunice | *Desperate Remedies* |
| Marian | *Tess of the D'Urbervilles* |
| Martha | *The Mayor of Casterbridge* |
| Martin, Mrs | *Two on a Tower* |
| Maybold, Parson, and his mother | *Under the Greenwood Tree* |
| Melbury, Grace | *The Woodlanders* |

209

## Characters

| | |
|---|---|
| Melburys, The – The first Mrs, George, Mrs Lucy | *The Woodlanders* |
| Menlove, Louisa | *The Hand of Ethelberta* |
| Mild, Lieutenant | *A Laodicean* |
| Millers, The – Soberness, Temperance | *Far From the Madding Crowd* |
| Mockridge, Nance | *The Mayor of Casterbridge* |
| Molly | *The Trumpet-Major* |
| Money, Maryann | *Far From the Madding Crowd* |
| Moon, Matthew | *Far From the Madding Crowd* |
| More, Jimmy | *A Laodicean* |
| Morris, Mrs | *Desperate Remedies* |
| Mountcleres, The Lord, Hon. Edgar | *The Hand of Ethelberta* |

### N

| | |
|---|---|
| Napper, Mrs | *The Hand of Ethelberta* |
| Neigh, Alfred | *The Hand of Ethelberta* |
| Newson, Elizabeth-Jane | *The Mayor of Casterbridge* |
| Newson, Richard | *The Mayor of Casterbridge* |
| Nobbs | *Two on a Tower* |
| Nunsuch, Susan, Johnny | *The Return of the Native* |

### O

| | |
|---|---|
| Oak, Gabriel | *Far From the Madding Crowd* |
| O'Fanagan, Mrs Tara | *The Hand of Ethelberta* |
| Oliver, Grammer | *The Woodlanders* |
| Orchard, Jane, Willy | *The Return of the Native* |
| Ounce, Captain | *The Hand of Ethelberta* |

### P

| | |
|---|---|
| Penny, Robert | *Under the Greenwood Tree* |
| Pennyways, Bailiff | *Far From the Madding Crowd* |
| Percomb, Mr | *The Woodlanders* |
| Perkins, Jane | *Far From the Madding Crowd* |
| Petherwin, Sir Ralph, and Lady, and their son | *The Hand of Ethelberta* |
| Phillotson, Richard | *Jude the Obscure* |

| | |
|---|---|
| Pierston, Isaac, Jocelyn | *The Well-Beloved* |
| Pine-Avon, Mrs Nichola | *The Well-Beloved* |
| Pitney, Mrs | *Tess of the D'Urbervilles* |
| Poorgrass, Joseph | *Far From the Madding Crowd* |
| Popp, Captain | *The Well-Beloved* |
| Power, Paula, Abner | *A Laodicean* |
| Priddle, Retty | *Tess of the D'Urbervilles* |

## R

| | |
|---|---|
| Rachel | *The Return of the Native* |
| Randall, Dan | *Far From the Madding Crowd* |
| Randle, Andrew | *Far From the Madding Crowd* |
| Raunham, Mr John | *Desperate Remedies* |
| Ravensbury, John | *A Laodicean* |
| Robin, Fanny | *Far From the Madding Crowd* |
| Rolliver, Mrs | *Tess of the D'Urbervilles* |
| Robert | *Desperate Remedies* |
| Rootle | *The Trumpet-Major* |
| Runt, Christopher | *Desperate Remedies* |
| Ryme, Joseph | *Under the Greenwood Tree* |

## S

| | |
|---|---|
| St Cleeves, The – Dr Jocelyn, The Rev., Swithin | *Two on a Tower* |
| Samway, Sam | *Far From the Madding Crowd* |
| Scribben, Sammy | *The Well-Beloved* |
| Seamore, Granny | *The Trumpet-Major* |
| Seaway, Anne | *Desperate Remedies* |
| Seedling, Amby | *Tess of the D'Urbervilles* |
| Shiner, Farmer Fred | *Under the Greenwood Tree* |
| Small, Mr | *The Hand of Ethelberta* |
| Smallburys, The – Andrew, Billy, Jacob, Joe, Lydday | *Far From the Madding Crowd* |
| Smiths, The – Mr and Mrs, Stephen | *A Pair of Blue Eyes* |
| Sneap, Luke | *Two on a Tower* |
| Sniff, Vashti | *Under the Greenwood Tree* |
| Somers, Alfred | *The Well-Beloved* |
| Somerset, George | *A Laodicean* |

## Characters

| | |
|---|---|
| South, John, Marty | *The Woodlanders* |
| Speedwell, Lady Iris | *The Well-Beloved* |
| Spinks, Elias | *Under the Greenwood Tree* |
| Springrove, Farmer and Mrs, and their son | *Desperate Remedies* |
| Stagg, Jack | *Jude the Obscure* |
| Stanner, Sergeant | *The Trumpet-Major* |
| Stannidge, Mr and Mrs | *The Mayor of Casterbridge* |
| Starks, Jim | *The Return of the Native* |
| Stockwool, Grammer | *The Well-Beloved* |
| Strickland, Captain | *The Hand of Ethelberta* |
| Strooden, Tim | *Desperate Remedies* |
| Stubb | *The Trumpet-Major* |
| Stubberd | *The Mayor of Casterbridge* |
| Swancourt, Rev. Christopher, Elfride, Charlotte | *A Pair of Blue Eyes* |

## T

| | |
|---|---|
| Tall, Susan, Laban | *Far From the Madding Crowd* |
| Tangs, Old Timothy, Young Timothy | *The Woodlanders* |
| Targe, Colonel, Elsie | *The Well-Beloved* |
| Templeman, Lucetta | *The Mayor of Casterbridge* |
| Tetuphenay, T. | *Jude the Obscure* |
| Thirdly, Parson | *Far From the Madding Crowd* |
| Timms, Mr | *Desperate Remedies* |
| Tipman | *The Hand of Ethelberta* |
| Torkingham, The Rev. | *Two on a Tower* |
| Traceley, Miss | *Jude the Obscure* |
| Tremlett, William | *The Trumpet-Major* |
| Trendle, Conjurer | *Tess of the D'Urbervilles* |
| Trewen, Mr and Mrs | *A Pair of Blue Eyes* |
| Tribble, Thomas | *The Hand of Ethelberta* |
| Tringham, Parson | *Tess of the D'Urbervilles* |
| Troutham, Farmer | *Jude the Obscure* |
| Troy, Sergeant Francis | *Far From the Madding Crowd* |
| Tullidge, Corporal | *The Trumpet-Major* |
| Twillis, Mrs | *Far From the Madding Crowd* |

## U

## V

## W

## Y

# FURTHER READING

For source-material on Hardy readers are advised to consult: *The Life of Thomas Hardy* by Florence Emily Hardy (1962); *Thomas Hardy's Personal Writings* edited Orel (1967); *The Architectural Notebooks of Thomas Hardy* edited C. J. P. Beatty (1966); *The Collected Letters of Thomas Hardy* edited Purdy and Millgate (Volume One published 1978, others to follow); *The Personal Notebooks of Thomas Hardy* edited R. H. Taylor (1978); *Some Recollections* by Emma Hardy, edited E. Hardy and R. Gittings (1961).

For biographical works: *Young Thomas Hardy* (1975) and *The Older Hardy* (1978) by Robert Gittings; *The First Mrs Hardy* by Denys Kay Robinson (1979); *The Second Mrs Hardy* by R. Gittings and J. Manton (1979). Michael Millgate is working on another full-scale biography. Other recommended books: *The Hardy Monographs* (Toucan Press), General editor J. Stevens Cox; *Talks with Thomas Hardy at Max Gate* by Vere H. Collins (1928); Virginia Woolf's fascinating account of her visit to Hardy in 1926 is contained in *A Writer's Diary* (1953) pp. 89–94; *Real Conversations* by William Archer (1904); *Letters* of T. E. Lawrence (1938).

There are many excellent book-length studies of Hardy's fiction. Especially recommended is the scholarly, informative *Thomas Hardy: his career as a novelist* by Michael Millgate (1971). Also *Thomas Hardy* by W. R. Rutland (1938); *Hardy the Novelist* by Lord David Cecil (1943); *Thomas Hardy* by Irving Howe (1967); *Thomas Hardy: Distance and Desire* by J. Hillis Miller (1970); *Hardy's Vision of Man* by F. R. Southerington (1971); *The Great Web* by Ian Gregor (1974). The best short study of Hardy is J. I. M. Stewart's in *Eight Modern Writers* (1963) and the same author's *Thomas Hardy: A Critical Biography* (1971), more critical than biographical, is elegant and witty.

Both the New Wessex and Penguin paperback editions of the novels contain helpful and expert introductions. Indeed, an excellent introduction to Hardy criticism may be found in Ronald Blythe's introductions to *A Pair of Blue Eyes* (New Wessex) or *Far From the Madding Crowd* (Penguin).

There are fine introductory essays to selections of Hardy's poetry by John Wain, P. N. Furbank, Geoffrey Grigson, James Gibson,

David Wright, G. M. Young. T. R. M. Creighton's *Poems of Thomas Hardy: A New Selection* (Revised edition, 1977) arranges the poems very effectively and provides excellent notes and commentary. Also recommended are J. O. Bailey's invaluable: *The Poetry of Thomas Hardy: A Handbook and Commentary* (1970); *Thomas Hardy and British Poetry* by Donald Davie (1973); *The Poems of Thomas Hardy: A Critical Introduction* by Kenneth Marsden (1969); *Thomas Hardy: the Poetry of Perception* by Tom Paulin (1975).

F. B. Pinion's *A Hardy Companion* (1968) is a helpful compendium covering all aspects of Hardy's life and work.

The standard bibliography is *Thomas Hardy: A Bibliographical Study* by R. L. Purdy (1954) – an outstanding contribution to Hardy studies giving useful biographical material as well as a comprehensive account of the genesis and publication of individual works.

Of the many other writings on Hardy I would like to recommend four more: D. H. Lawrence's remarkable *Study of Thomas Hardy* (1936); Roy Morrell's personal and challenging *Thomas Hardy: The Will and the Way* (1965); Raymond Williams' chapter on Hardy in *The English Novel from Dickens to Lawrence* (1970); John Bayley's *An Essay on Thomas Hardy* (1978) – a masterly study which constantly puts the reader in contact with Hardy's text.